"Until you make the unconscious conscious, it will direct your life and you will call it fate."

— *Carl Jung*

Contents

Section I: Awareness of the Field

1. Metaphysical Biology 2
2. You Are Electromagnetic 5
3. You Are The Signal 8
4. Aura Mechanics 11
5. Heart Intelligence 17
6. The Listening Body 20
7. Magnified Emotion 23
8. The Subconscious Operator 26
9. Wanting vs. Resonating 30
10. Reflective Reality 33

Section II: Frequency Mechanics

1. Thought Into Form 40
2. The Belief Layer 43
3. Signal Interference 46
4. Frequency Calibration 49
5. The Emotion Trap 52
6. Embodied Frequency 56
7. The Law of Resonance 59
8. Energetic Gravity 62
9. Energy Manipulation 71

Contents

Section III: External Navigation

1. *Field Dynamics* 75

2. *Reality Feedback Loops* 78

3. *Energetic Leakage* 81

4. *Relational Frequency* 84

5. *Environmental Frequency* 87

Section IV: The Creation Protocol

1. *The Instruction Loop* 92

2. *Frequency Mastery* 95

3. *Collapse as Calibration* 98

4. *Command State* 101

5. *The Operator Identity* 104

6. *Imagination Protocol* 107

Conclusion:

1. *The Remembering* 111

(ACT)

DISCLAIMER

*THE CONTENTS OF THIS BOOK ARE INTENDED FOR INFORMATIONAL
AND EDUCATIONAL PURPOSES ONLY AND ARE NOT INTENDED AS
MEDICAL, PSYCHOLOGICAL, LEGAL, OR FINANCIAL ADVICE.
THE AUTHOR MAKES NO GUARANTEES OF SPECIFIC RESULTS, AS
OUTCOMES WILL VARY DEPENDING ON THE READER'S PERSONAL
CHOICES, BELIEFS, AND INTERPRETATIONS.*

*By reading this book, you acknowledge that you are responsible for
your own decisions and experiences. This book does not replace
professional guidance or treatment, and should not be used as a
substitute for qualified advice from licensed professionals.*

*The concepts discussed herein explore metaphysical and energetic
perspectives that are not recognized by conventional science or
medicine. The author makes no claims regarding the
empirical verifiability of these perspectives.*

*All content is provided in good faith and is the result of the author's
personal experience, research, and interpretation. Readers are
encouraged to approach this material with discernment and
personal responsibility.*

I didn't invent The Frequency Effect.

I remembered it,
across time, pattern, and presence.

In ancient systems disguised as symbols.

In the quiet cadence of those who had
mastered reality without noise.

I kept tracing the same current,
beneath belief, beneath language.

It wasn't mystical in nature.

It only seemed that way until you
saw how exact it really was.

There's an architecture behind
every outcome.

A rhythm behind every result.

A frequency behind every choice.

Not something new.
Something forgotten.

This isn't a method.
It's a memory.

A remembering of how thought
actually becomes form.

Once you see it,
you stop chasing change.

You begin creating it.

- Beau Harlem
Founder of Accurate Thought

Before You Begin...

This book isn't for skimming.
It's built for repetition and real use.

What's inside isn't theory.

These pages outline the structural mechanics
behind thought, energy, and reality, meant to
be worked with, not just read.

You won't get it all at once, and that's
intentional.

Each reread drives the system deeper, building
new links in your subconscious and clarifying
patterns for actual change.

This is deliberate recalibration, not passive
consumption.

Some sections will challenge you; others will
confirm what you already know underneath.

Either way, it's up to you to engage, revisit,
and let the material reshape your internal
framework.

Take your time. This Isn't about blind
acceptance, it's about building real awareness
and applying it.

Read carefully. Return often. Let each concept
do its work.

This isn't information, it's a tool for
reprogramming how you operate.

The more you engage, the more your reality
will reflect it.

"To live in the world without becoming aware of the meaning of the world is like wandering about in a great library without touching the books."

— *Manly P. Hall*

SECTION I: AWARENESS OF THE FIELD

Your body is surrounded by an electromagnetic field, commonly called the "aura." This isn't a concept. It's measurable and it's not fixed. It changes continuously, adjusting to your internal state. It responds to feeling, the deep, sustained resonance you carry beneath thought.

Feeling creates frequency. And frequency sends instruction. This is "as within, so without" applied at the energetic level.

Your emotional state isn't contained inside you. It radiates outward and organizes the space around you. Your electromagnetic field moves in a precise pattern: a self-sustaining loop of energy known as the torus.

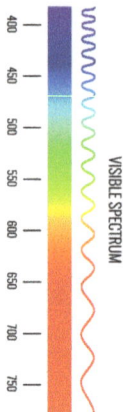

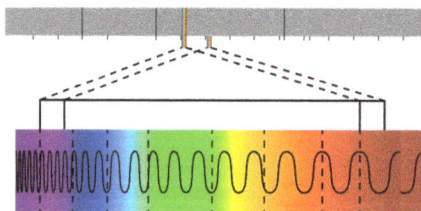

This torus begins at your heart. It spirals upward, out through the crown, wraps around your body, and re-enters from below. It's not symbolic, it's structural. Your energy moves in this exact pattern. And in doing so, it communicates with the quantum field around you.

The mechanism: Your torus is your broadcast system. It holds charge. It sends signal. Its frequency is shaped by two forces: what you feel consistently, and what you focus on continuously.

This is why two people can share the same world and live entirely different experiences. Each field is sending different instructions. Same room, different reality. The signal being broadcast is different.

Your electromagnetic field doesn't just attract. It filters experience through resonance. As your frequency shifts, your reality changes with it, bringing new thoughts, people, and outcomes. This isn't about thinking positively. It's about regulating your internal state so the external world responds.

Think of it like tuning a radio. You don't attract the music, you tune to the frequency that's already broadcasting. Change the frequency, and the content changes instantly. Manifestation begins with frequency, and frequency begins in the body. Not the visible form, but the energy it emits through thought, emotion, and belief. Your nervous system, heart, and field function as one transmitter. When the signal is aligned, the environment reflects it.

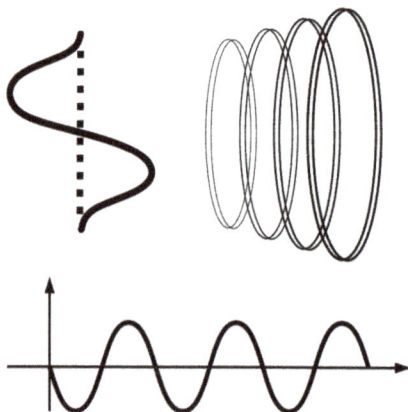

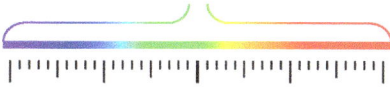

Your heart is the central generator of your electromagnetic field, emitting more electrical power than the brain and carrying its own intelligence.

The heart's electromagnetic field is 60 times stronger than the brain's electrical field and 5,000 times stronger magnetically.

Its rhythm shapes brainwaves, hormones, and emotion. When coherent, its field becomes stronger and more organized. This coherence is created through feeling. Gratitude, calm, and certainty produce smooth, powerful rhythms that amplify your field, while stress and fear distort it. Your heart isn't just a muscle. It's a tuning fork.

Beneath your awareness, your nervous system is always listening. It reacts to every thought you sustain, every belief you accept, every emotion you resist or release.

This is how thought becomes biology.

Your nervous system doesn't distinguish between imagined and real. It only responds to signal. If you imagine failure while feeling fear, your body produces cortisol and broadcasts survival. If you imagine success while feeling certainty, your body produces oxytocin and broadcasts coherence.

What begins as a thought eventually becomes a state. And every state creates a unique frequency pattern in the field.

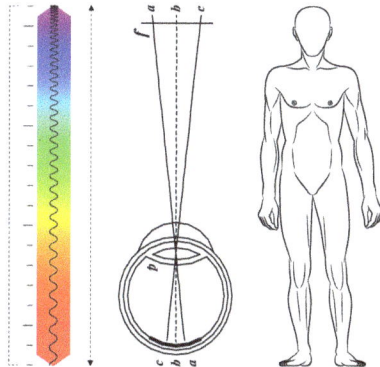

The energy you carry is not just motion. It leaves a trail. The more you repeat a state, the more prominent the imprint. That imprint becomes part of your field's baseline. And your baseline determines what you resonate with.

This is why change feels slow. Energy patterns are reinforced by habit. Your nervous system has been running the same loops for years. But the moment a new emotional state is held with clarity and consistency, the imprint begins to change.

Biology listens. The field listens. Reality listens. You don't need years of work. You need to hold a new frequency consistently until it becomes your baseline. That's the recipe.

METAPHYSICAL BIOLOGY

*You are not just
thinking thoughts.*

**You are sending
instructions**.

The way you feel,

the way you breathe,

the way you focus.

It all shapes your field.

*Your biology is not
holding you back.*

*It is waiting for **your
direction**.*

*And once you begin to
direct it consciously,*

*the laws of reality start
responding with
precision.*

YOU ARE THE BIOLOGY

SET THE FREQUENCY. INITIATE THE SIGNAL.

Clarify your internal baseline:

- *What emotional state are you currently operating from?*

....

....

....

....

- *What thoughts or insights come up as you notice this?*

....

....

....

....

Example prompts:
- *I operate from certainty, no mixed frequency.*
- *My system runs calm, not chaos.*
- *I'm not waiting for clarity. I'm generating it.*
- *My field is locked to direction, not emotion.*

You do not stop at your skin.
Your electromagnetic field extends beyond the body and into the space around you. It moves with you, responds to you, and reflects the state you carry.

This field is not imagined. It's real, active, and measurable. And it's through this field that your presence is felt. You may speak calmly, but if your field is tense, others will feel the tension. You may smile, but if your field carries grief, it's still transmitted.

This is how people sense each other beyond words.

It's not intuition.
It's energy.

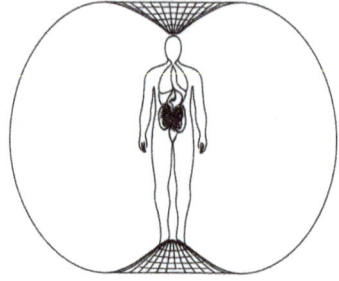

$$\mathcal{E} = -\frac{d\Phi}{dt}$$

(Faraday's Law reveals that a shifting magnetic field generates an electric force, and the faster the shift, the stronger the response, always pushing back against the change that created it).

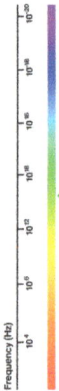

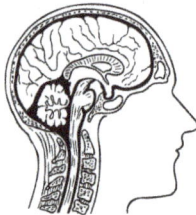

The brain produces electric impulses. The heart generates an even stronger electromagnetic charge. Together, they create the energetic signature you send into space.

That signature is shaped by what you think and powered by what you feel. Thoughts give the field form. Emotions give it strength.

When the two are aligned, your field becomes coherent, steady, focused, and influential. When they're out of sync, your signal fragments. And with that fragmentation, experience becomes inconsistent.

You've felt this disruption before.
Moments when nothing quite lands, no matter how hard you try. You feel uncertain. Disconnected.

You question your thoughts or your instincts. But often it's not your thoughts that are off. It's your field.

When your internal state lacks structure, the space around you responds in kind.

Situations feel harder to control.
People misunderstand you.
The signal is fuzzy, and reality reflects it.

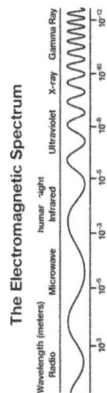

5

Thousands of experiments over the past century have confirmed the Schrödinger Equation

$$-\hbar^2/2m\,\nabla^2\Psi + V\Psi = i\hbar\partial\Psi/\partial t$$

(This equation predicts how quantum systems change over time, with unmatched accuracy. It proves that reality unfolds as probability waves, shaped by observation).

When the field becomes clear again, things start to click. You feel grounded in your body and sharp in your awareness. You speak and are heard. You move and feel supported. There's no reaching, no gripping, only presence.

This isn't luck or timing. It's coherence.

Your thoughts, emotions, and intentions are in rhythm.

And the world organizes around that rhythm. The field becomes magnetic, and reality adjusts accordingly.

Most people don't realize they're broadcasting. They respond to their environment without noticing that they're influencing it.

They feel drained, overwhelmed, or out of sync. and blame the world. But the field is active, not neutral.

It doesn't just record your state. It projects it. And everything you encounter reflects that projection.

Until you become aware of what you're carrying, the world will keep showing it to you in different forms.

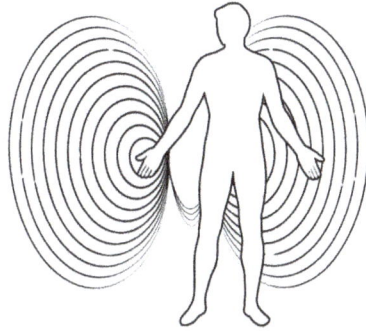

(Nikola Tesla understood that frequency is the foundation of all form, long before quantum physics proved that reality itself is structured by vibration, not matter).

This awareness is the foundation of change. You are not just thinking through life. You are signaling through it.

Every thought, every breath, every feeling you sustain adds to the broadcast. You don't need to force outcomes when your field is aligned.
You shape them through clarity, consistency, and internal order.

The electromagnetic self is not a metaphor. It's the part of you that reality responds to most. And the more you feel it, the more you can use it.

YOU ARE ELECTROMAGNETIC

You are not just experiencing life.

You are broadcasting into it.

Every internal shift in thought, emotion, or focus changes what the field around you carries.

Your energy is not fixed. **It is responsive.**

The moment you begin to feel yourself as a signal, rather than a self-contained mind, you step into the role **you were built for.**

Not reacting to reality.

Shaping it.

You are not just surrounded by a field.

You are actively transmitting into one.

Every thought you think, every emotion you feel, every belief you hold creates a vibrational signature. And that signature doesn't stay inside you. It enters the quantum field, the space where all possibilities exist before they take form.

This field has been called many names: the ether, the zero point field, the unified field. The term doesn't matter. What matters is understanding that it's real, active, and responsive.

(Your body is the union of earth, water, fire, air, and ether, five elements expressed as five living fingers).

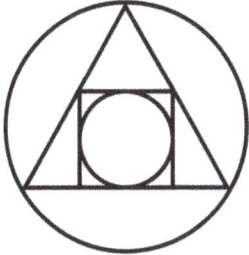

(This symbol represents the integration of spirit, mind, and matter, the core elements that combine to form reality as a whole.)

This field operates on a principle called superposition. In quantum mechanics, particles exist in all possible states simultaneously until they are observed. Observation collapses the wave function and brings one specific outcome into form.

You are the observer. Your frequency is the observation. And the field responds by collapsing probability into experience that matches your signal.

You're not creating something from nothing. You're selecting from infinite possibility by tuning to a specific frequency. Everything already exists in potential. Your signal determines which version becomes real.

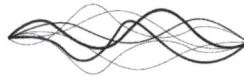

Your signal is not just what you consciously think. It's what you subconsciously believe, emotionally embody, and energetically broadcast.
Most people think one thing, feel another, and believe something entirely different.

The field doesn't interpret intention. It reads frequency. If you say "I want success" but feel unworthy, the field responds to unworthiness, not the words. If you visualize abundance but carry a frequency of lack, lack is what returns. The signal must be coherent. Thought, emotion, and belief aligned into one clear frequency. Only then does the field have a consistent instruction to follow.

The zero point field is not bound by time.

It exists outside of linear progression. This is why your signal can influence outcomes before they physically appear. When you shift your frequency, the field responds instantly. But matter takes time to reorganize.

Physical reality moves slower than energy. The delay you experience is not in the field's response. It's in how long it takes for the material world to catch up to your new signal.

This gap exists because you must hold your frequency steady long enough for the physical plane to mirror your energetic state.

This is why patterns repeat.
Because the field remains tuned to what you haven't yet changed. Until the broadcast shifts, the feedback loop stays active.

The ether is always listening.
It holds no opinion.
It only reflects what you send.
And the moment your signal becomes clear, your timeline begins to bend.

New outcomes emerge.
Not because of luck.

Because of resonance.

You are not sending energy into space.
You are shaping the space itself.
You live inside a responsive field that reorganizes reality based on your internal state.

You don't have to force the world to change.
You only have to become coherent within it.
The clearer your signal, the faster the field can respond.

And once you realize that your signal enters the space where all things begin, you stop waiting for permission.
You start broadcasting with purpose.

YOU ARE THE SIGNAL

*You are not separate
from the space you
move through.*

You are informing it.

*Every thought you
hold, every emotion
you embody,
every belief you
reinforce, becomes
part of the broadcast.*

*You're not waiting for
reality to shift.*

*You are shaping the
field it emerges from.*

*And once your signal
becomes steady and
clear, the ether has
no choice but to
respond.*

Not someday.
But now.

YOU ARE THE SIGNAL

ANCHOR YOUR FREQUENCY. BROADCAST THE OUTCOME.

Describe your signal clearly:

- *What are you embodying right now?*

....

....

....

....

- *What thoughts, feelings, and intentions define this?*

....

....

....

....

Example prompts:
- *I radiate confidence and attract success naturally.*
- *I create reality with clear, focused intention.*
- *My energy draws supportive and meaningful connections.*
- *I move through each day with purpose and control.*

The torus is not a theory, it's a blueprint.

From atomic fields to galactic spirals, the toroidal loop shows up across every scale of nature.

It is self-sustaining, regenerative, and efficient. In the human body, this field radiates from the heart and forms a continuous loop: upward through the crown, around the body, and back in through the base.

It's measurable, and once understood, it becomes usable. The torus is nature's most efficient energy structure. It continuously recycles energy through a central axis. No energy is lost. It feeds itself.

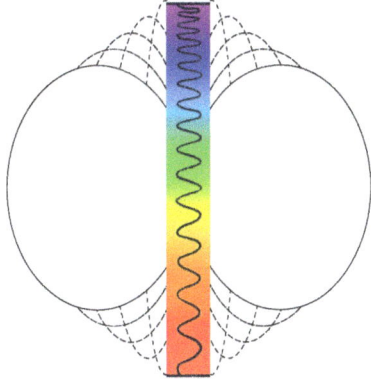

Ancient symbols captured this structure long before modern science. The vesica piscis, two overlapping circles creating an almond-shaped center, is a direct cross-section of the torus.

Found in Egyptian, Hindu, and Christian art, it represented the womb of creation. Similarly, the Sri Yantra maps this flow through interlocking geometry, spiraling in and out like the toroidal field.

These weren't decorations. They were functional models encoded into visual form. Temples, mandalas, and sacred geometry weren't art for its own sake. They were blueprints for how energy moves through consciousness and reality.

The Tree of Life in Kabbalah depicts energy moving in recursive patterns, descent and ascent, across ten spheres.

This mirrors the energetic loop of the torus within the body. Energy doesn't move in a straight line. It cycles.

What you send out through intention returns through form.

This is not mysticism. It's how frequency interacts with the field. And mystics across cultures used breath, posture, and resonance to regulate this current on command.

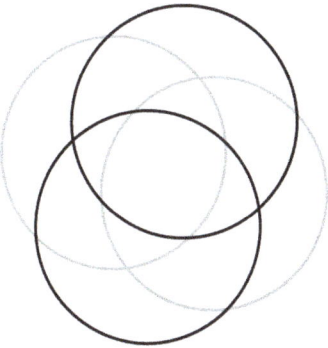

Your aura is the visible trace of this toroidal field in motion.

Above your crown, it spirals out, often reflected in the growth pattern of your hair.

Each layer of the field maps to a level of consciousness: physical, emotional, mental, spiritual. These aren't symbolic terms. They're energetic bands.

When internal conflict or emotional distortion disrupts these layers, the torus weakens. And when it weakens, life stops responding with precision. Field integrity is everything.

Architecture once reflected this awareness. Circular temples, domed ceilings, and spiral staircases weren't just aesthetic choices, they aligned with the natural flow of energy.

Structures like Stonehenge and ancient ziggurats harnessed proportion and geometry to amplify resonance, working in sync with the same toroidal rhythm emitted by the human energy field.

These weren't simply places of worship or ceremony. They were engineered to influence internal states, tools for restoring field coherence and expansion.

(The Great Pyramid of Giza harnesses energy from the Earth's electromagnetic field).
The King's Chamber is centered in a way that aligns with zero-point harmonics, toroidal resonance.

(Structures like Stonehenge, with their circular form and central point, embody the toroidal current. Each stone acts as a resonant marker, attuned to Earth's magnetic grid and anchoring planetary toroidal energy).

You are not just inside this torus, you generate and refine it. Breath recharges its current. Feeling stabilizes its spin. Thought aligns its orientation.

As your inner state becomes more coherent, the field strengthens, patterns become more efficient, and interference drops. This is when outcomes begin to change, not from pressure or willpower, but from synchronization.

The torus is not passive background architecture. It is an active mirror. The cleaner the signal you send, the more directly reality reflects your internal structure back to you.

AURA MECHANICS

*Your aura is the outer layer of **your energy system**.*

*It reflects your current state and **stores** traces of past emotions, trauma, and beliefs.*

*Each loop of the torus acts as a feedback cycle, pulling in new energy and **broadcasting your frequency.***

When coherent, the aura becomes stable and precise.
When disordered, the field fragments.

This isn't symbolic,

*it's a practical interface with the field **shaping your experience**.*

TORUS
SYMBOLOGY

THE ELECTROMAGNETIC FIELD.

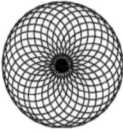   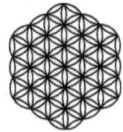

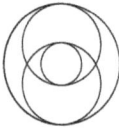   

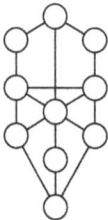  

THE TORUS IN
nature

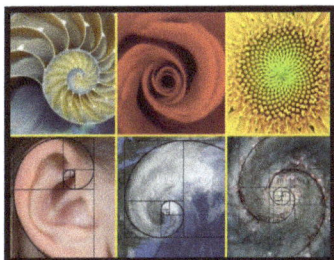

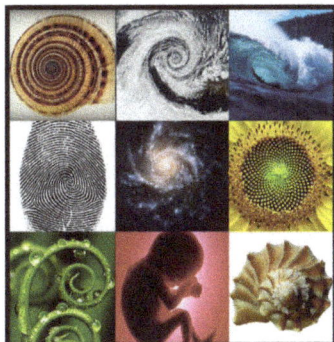

THE ATOM

The true atom is not a particle, it's a field. Specifically, an electromagnetic toroidal field. Energy spiraling inward and outward through a central axis, self-generating, self-sustaining.

This is the blueprint beneath matter.

In ancient Egypt, they said "All is Atum." Not a god. A unified field. They understood what modern science is only now confirming: everything arises from a single, living energy. Matter is just condensed frequency.

That's why Tesla said, "If you want to understand the secrets of the universe, think in terms of energy, frequency, and vibration."

He wasn't being poetic. His 3-6-9 was a map of how energy expands. Three represents energy in its raw form. Six is that energy organized into frequency. Nine is frequency manifested as vibration, the physical expression.

It's the sequence of creation itself.
Energy becomes frequency.
Frequency becomes form.

The heart is not just an organ that pumps blood. It is the central conductor of your electromagnetic field, the primary source of rhythm and coherence in the body.

Unlike the brain, which generates low-voltage electrical signals, the heart emits a powerful, measurable field that extends several feet beyond the skin. This isn't abstract. It's measurable in real-time using magnetometers.

Through this broadcast, the heart serves as your biological interface with the field around you, regulating the structure, strength, and clarity of your electromagnetic presence.

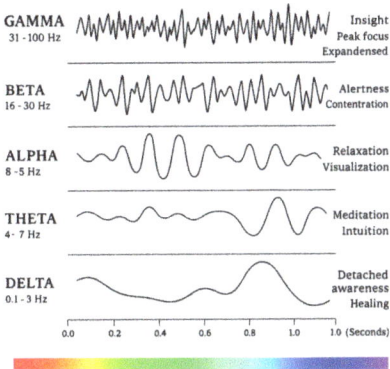

Heart intelligence refers to the regulatory intelligence that emerges when the heart's rhythm becomes coherent.

In this state, the heart sends synchronized instructions to the nervous system, affecting hormone release, brainwave patterns, and overall system balance. Coherence isn't just calmness, it's electrical efficiency.

In coherence, fewer signals are wasted, and more energy is directed. This improves reaction time, decision quality, and emotional stability. The more consistently you access this state, the less friction appears between intention and outcome.

Most people attempt change through mental force, using thought to override feeling. But in the absence of coherence, even clear thoughts lose power. The signal weakens.

Coherence is what amplifies thought into effect. And coherence is tuned by emotion, not intellect. States like appreciation, calm, and trust optimize the heart's rhythm.

They clean the waveform, reducing distortion. On the other hand, urgency, resentment, or doubt introduce irregularity, sending out chaotic frequencies that disrupt outcomes. It's not personal, it's pattern-based.

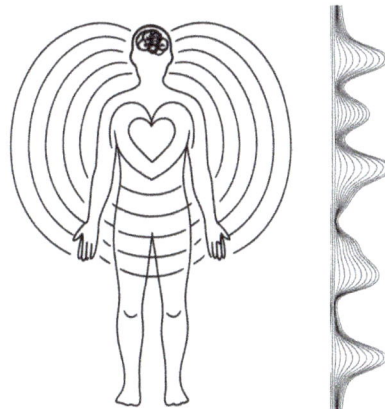

When the heart is coherent, the field becomes organized. Patterns of interaction improve. Situations become more fluid. Communication sharpens.

This is alignment, not as a spiritual idea, but as a systemic upgrade in how internal states interact with external variables.

In ancient systems, the heart sat above the brain because it governed reality. Egyptians weighed it against a feather, not for morality, but to represent enlightenment: a state beyond reactive emotion, where internal balance shaped external outcome.

Coherence can't be forced. It has to be entered.
You don't get there by overthinking, you get there through presence and regulation.

Awareness, not pressure, shifts the rhythm of the heart. The more you practice entering this state deliberately, the more your body defaults to it.

And when that shift becomes your baseline, the world starts responding differently, not to who you try to be, but to what your field continuously emits.

(Christ points upward, signaling that higher states are reached not through thought, but through the heart, feeling is the bridge to elevated vibration).

Heart intelligence is the conversion point between thought and frequency, the translator between idea and reality. When it's active, your output becomes more precise.

You stop reacting from emotional noise and start broadcasting direction. This is not a passive organ. It's an intelligent generator.

And once trained, it becomes your most efficient tool for interfacing with the field around you.

It doesn't push. It doesn't force. It sets the signal. And everything else follows.

HEART INTELLIGENCE

*Your heart is more
than emotion, it's your
**strongest magnetic
transmitter**.*

*It shapes your field,
which shapes your
experience.*

*Calm and gratitude
bring coherence.
Stress and doubt
scatter the signal.*

*This isn't mysticism,
it's measurable.
Your emotional state
influences what shows
up.*

*Heart intelligence
means holding that
coherence,
so life can reflect it
back, without force.*

Coherence begins in the heart, but it's the subconscious mind that holds the program.

Thought can spark change, but only the subconscious makes it last. Until it accepts the signal, your body keeps broadcasting the old one. The subconscious governs your default state, and it doesn't respond to isolated thoughts. It responds to repetition combined with emotion.

Only then does it begin to accept the new pattern as real. This is the requirement: Thought must be charged by emotion to reach the subconscious.

The subconscious doesn't judge. It stores. Whatever emotion you rehearse most often becomes the rule it follows.

That's what makes autosuggestion effective.
It's not about saying something over and over, but feeling it as you say it.

Emotion is the delivery mechanism, it decides whether a thought is ignored or integrated.

If the feeling doesn't match the thought, the body won't believe it and keeps broadcasting the old pattern.

Once a thought reaches the subconscious, the nervous system begins to adapt.

Your reactions shift. Your posture changes. Without needing to force it, your presence starts reflecting the new internal pattern. This is how a new baseline is created, not through effort, but through repetition.

When that pattern stabilizes, it becomes what's known as "unconscious competence".

With enough emotional reinforcement, the belief takes root, and the body begins responding as if it's already true. And because the field reflects what the body broadcasts consistently, your external reality starts to respond in kind.

Most people try to install new thoughts while still running old emotions. But the subconscious doesn't listen to ideas, it listens to patterns.

And if the emotional pattern doesn't match the new belief, the old one stays active. To change the signal, both thought and feeling must align.

When the image in your mind and the emotion in your body agree, the subconscious accepts the suggestion. And once it's accepted, it begins reinforcing that signal automatically.

That reinforcement shows up as a new frequency. Your responses vibrate differently. You speak with cleaner signal. You move with less static.

The energy you emit becomes stable, because the body is no longer reacting to old data. It's transmitting a new instruction. This is embodiment, not as an idea, but as a measurable shift in frequency.

And once your system holds that signal consistently, the field no longer reads it as potential, it reads it as origin.

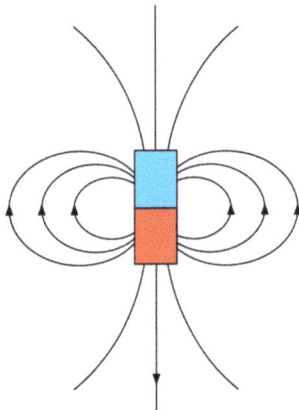

The subconscious is always broadcasting. It doesn't transmit what's logical, it transmits what's familiar.

Every repeated thought, every emotional charge, every state you sustain builds your frequency profile.

When your mental focus aligns with your emotional tone, and your nervous system begins reinforcing that vibration, you create coherence across the entire signal.

And once coherence locks in, mind, body, and field, the return signal from reality begins to accelerate.

THE LISTENING BODY

The subconscious
doesn't hear words.

It hears signals.

And those signals
are shaped by what
you feel most often.

When emotion
reinforces thought,
**the body starts to
believe it.**

That belief becomes
a new pattern,
held without effort.

You're not forcing
change.

You're tuning it.

The field doesn't
react to effort.

**It responds to
coherence.**

THE LISTENING BODY

ALIGN THOUGHT AND EMOTION. SET THE PATTERN.

Input your current signal:

- *What reality are you currently broadcasting through belief?*

....

....

....

....

- *What emotional state is actively reinforcing that signal?*

....

....

....

....

Example prompts:
- *I move as if the outcome is inevitable, the signal reflects it.*
- *My baseline is built on stability, and the field is matching it.*
- *The belief is installed. The feeling confirms it.*
- *I'm not projecting hope, I'm transmitting certainty.*

Emotion is energy. Every feeling you hold shifts your system. It changes how your body signals, and how the field responds.

It influences heart rhythm, brain coherence, hormonal output, and field strength.
This energy becomes part of your electromagnetic broadcast.

The more consistently an emotional state is experienced, the more it begins to influence your subconscious baseline.
But that doesn't happen from intensity alone.
It happens through repetition.
The subconscious only accepts what becomes familiar. Until then, it reverts to the emotional patterns it already trusts.

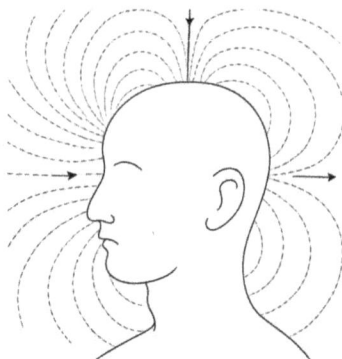

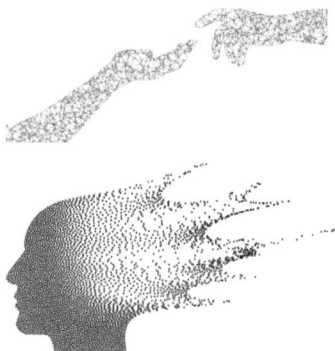

You can think about something you want, but if you feel doubt while thinking it, you're not reinforcing the goal, you're reinforcing the doubt.

To the subconscious, the emotional tone carries more weight than the image itself. This means a thought paired with frustration or fear is not moving you toward the outcome.

It's reinforcing the belief that the outcome is out of reach.

What you feel while thinking is what the system records. Not the goal, the charge behind it.

This is why most people unknowingly reinforce the wrong pattern.

They focus on improvement, but the emotional charge behind their focus is resistance.
The body tightens. The breath shortens. The nervous system responds as if the goal is a threat.
Even if the words are about success, the signal being sent is avoidance, fear, or self-rejection. The subconscious doesn't distinguish between desire and discomfort.

It encodes whatever is repeated with emotion. And if that emotion is negative, the imprint will match it, not the intention.

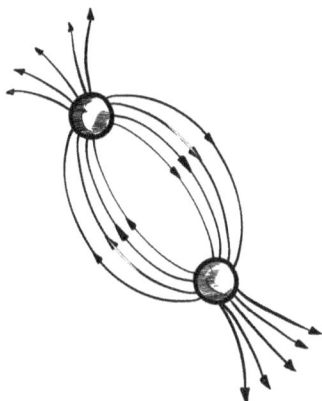

Emotion is energy in motion, and that motion creates momentum. High-charge emotions like calm, confidence, and trust create internal coherence.

They organize your nervous system, stabilize your field, and improve your ability to hold a consistent signal. That stability is what allows outcomes to shift.

On the other hand, low-charge states like guilt, self-doubt, or urgency fragment the signal. They introduce inconsistency, not just mentally, but energetically. And because the field reflects whatever is most consistent, it begins returning the vibration of conflict, not clarity.

Your system is shaped by what you feel repeatedly. The subconscious doesn't update from information. It updates from reinforced emotional states. Whatever emotion is rehearsed most often, whether intentional or unconscious, becomes the dominant instruction to your body and your field.

The nervous system needs repetition. One thought doesn't rewire the field. A new state, felt often enough, does.

Only then does the subconscious begin accepting it as normal. And once it's accepted, it becomes easier to maintain.

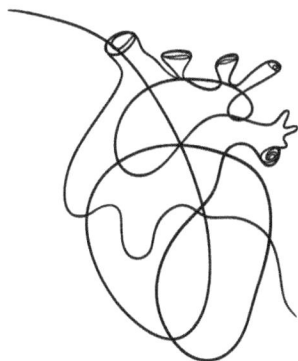

This is the purpose of the upcoming Field Imprint exercise. It gives your system a clear instruction: Here is the identity. Here is the emotional state. Here is the outcome that follows.

By repeating that alignment often enough, the emotion becomes familiar, and the subconscious begins to adopt it. Once the body adjusts to the new state and holds it without resistance, the field mirrors that adjustment back into your external life. This is not placebo. It's how emotion modifies the field, and how field modifies experience.

Thought creates structure. Emotion powers it. And when both are aligned consistently, the field changes.

MAGNIFIED EMOTION

*Emotion is not
the side effect,*
it's the amplifier.

*It tells the field
how serious you
are.*

*Whatever you feel
most intensely*
**becomes
instruction.**

*That's why fear
loops, and that's
why joy expands.*

*Your frequency is
not just what you
think,*

**It's what you
energize.**

MAGNIFIED EMOTION

INTENSIFY THE SIGNAL. LOCK IN THE STATE.

Define your amplified emotional state:

- *What powerful emotion are you consistently running right now?*

....

....

....

....

- *What focus or intention is helping that emotion stay active?*

....

....

....

....

Example prompts:
- *I amplify calm power, I'm not rushing, I'm receiving.*
- *I'm holding desire, but without resistance or lack.*
- *I'm grounded in trust, my system no longer second-guesses.*
- *I'm sustaining momentum, the feeling of progress keeps the loop active.*

The subconscious is not passive. It's active, always running, always filtering, always reinforcing.

It governs over 90% of your decisions, reactions, and perception without asking for permission. It's not trying to sabotage you. It's trying to maintain internal consistency.

Whatever emotional states and beliefs have been repeated most often are treated as "safe" even if they're unwanted.

This means the subconscious doesn't guide you toward what's best. It guides you toward what's familiar.

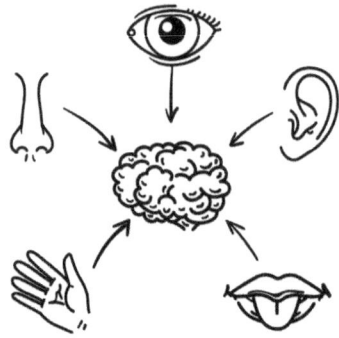

You don't see reality as it is. You see it as your subconscious expects it to be.

It filters your attention, edits your perception, and influences your response all before you consciously process what's happening.

If your system is imprinted with fear, it will scan for threat. If it's imprinted with lack, it will ignore opportunity.

This happens automatically. Not because you're broken, but because the subconscious is built to protect, not evolve.

The subconscious works like a predictive program. It receives information from the body, compares it to stored emotional memory, and chooses behavior based on the closest match.

It doesn't evaluate your future. It plays back your past unless you intervene.

This is why emotional patterns repeat. Not because life is against you, but because your signal hasn't changed.

The subconscious keeps executing the same instruction because that's what the system has confirmed as "normal."

Your signal is shaped by the subconscious baseline. You might consciously want change, but if your body is still reacting from old emotional memory, the output won't match the intention.

This creates internal conflict, one part of you is reaching forward, while another part is broadcasting backward.

Until the subconscious receives a new pattern, repeatedly and clearly, it will continue defaulting to what it knows. And because your field is built from the signal your body sends, the results don't shift until the programming does.

This is not about blame. This is about responsibility.

The subconscious isn't permanent, it's programmable. But it doesn't respond to hope or willpower. It responds to emotional repetition, internal consistency, and signals that become more familiar than the ones they replace.

Once a new signal is installed often enough, the subconscious begins to favor it. And when it favors it, the nervous system aligns. Your reactions change. Your field changes. And the world reflects it because the instruction is now different.

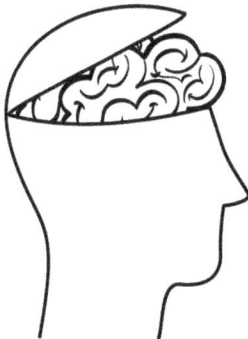

This is why coherence matters. A clear signal held consistently over time becomes the dominant instruction. It doesn't happen in a single moment. It happens through emotional conditioning. That's what rewrites the subconscious operator.

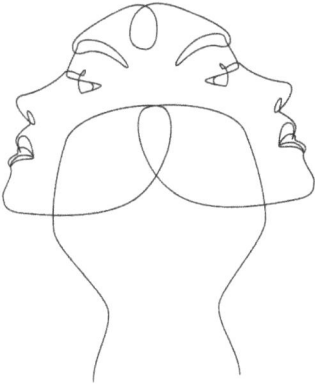

You are not fighting against your mind. You are re-training it to serve a new identity. And as that identity becomes familiar, the subconscious will begin running it without resistance.

When that happens, the system is no longer reinforcing the past. It's projecting the future through signal.

THE SUBCONSCIOUS OPERATOR

*The subconscious
is not passive,*

it's in command.

*It runs the signal
beneath every
decision.*

*You don't need to
control it.*

**You need to
train it.**

*Repetition with
emotion writes
the code.*

*And once the
code is set,*

**the field
responds
automatically.**

IMPRINT THE FIELD

ANCHOR YOUR FREQUENCY. BROADCAST THE OUTCOME.

IDENTITY SIGNAL

(Who are you becoming? Write it as if it's already true.)

I AM ....

I AM ....

THE OUTCOME CARD

Cut it out, paste it somewhere common. Imprint your field. Use this card as a daily reference to hold the outcome in mind and emotion, until it becomes familiar.

(Write as if it is already happening. Be clear, not vague.)

....

....

....

Example prompts:
- *I attract aligned opportunities without effort.*
- *I lead a business that grows on command.*
- *My relationships mirror the peace I've become.*
- *I wake up clear, focused, and fully in charge.*

Most people don't realize that wanting something and resonating with it are not the same.

You can visualize an outcome, write it down, and think about it daily yet still repel it.
Wanting often isn't alignment.
It's a signal of absence.

The subconscious doesn't respond to your words. It responds to your emotional tone.
And when that tone is lack, the field mirrors it.
Not because it's cruel, but because that's the signal you're sending.
It doesn't deliver outcomes based on ideas.
It reflects the emotional broadcast your system emits most consistently.

Desire alone doesn't create change.

If you think about what you want while feeling frustrated or doubtful, you're reinforcing the gap, not bridging it.
The subconscious hears the feeling, not the thought.

It organizes your system around what's emotionally dominant.

If the emotion is "I don't have this," then that becomes your energetic instruction.
So the result remains out of reach, not due to lack of intention, but because of emotional misalignment.

Resonance is different.

It means your internal state already matches the outcome. You don't need to chase it, you begin to feel it now.

You generate the emotion of already having it, which installs a new frequency.

The subconscious recognizes the feeling as familiar and updates the baseline. Once it accepts this as normal, your nervous system stops rejecting it.

Then the field returns that signal, not because you forced it, but because you became it.

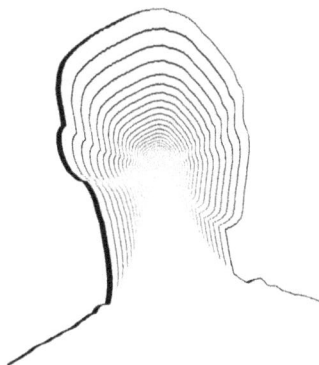

The field doesn't follow effort.
It follows instruction.

Instruction is carried by emotion.
If your dominant tone is lack, you'll keep
receiving situations that match it.

This isn't punishment. It's precision.

The field mirrors what your system
broadcasts, not what your mind hopes for.

Until you emit the frequency of already
having, the result stays outside your
experience. Matching begins internally. The
field only plays back what you send out.

This is where many people stay stuck.

They visualize, affirm, and study but remain emotionally in "not there yet."
And that becomes the signal.

Their body broadcasts lack while their mind
projects goals.

But the field listens to the stronger signal.
And emotion always wins.

Your body language, decisions, and energy
speak louder than your intentions.

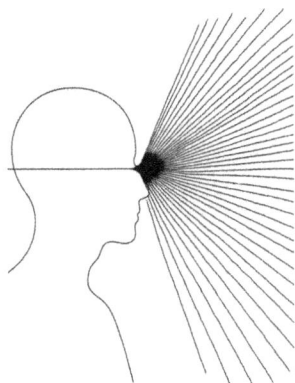

To resonate, stop reaching. Instead, train your
system to feel the result as real now.

This isn't pretending, it's pattern installation.

Top performers already live here.
They don't hope. They expect.
Certainty has become their default.
So reality organizes around it.

They operate from internal alignment before
action, not after results. When that emotion
stabilizes, your subconscious accepts it. The field
adjusts because the signal now says it's already
done.

WANTING VS. RESONATING

Desire alone doesn't move the field.
Resonance does.

Wanting signals absence.

Resonating broadcasts ***alignment.***

When the body holds the feeling of already having, ***the field mirrors that instruction.***

Not because you tried harder, but because you stopped sending mixed signals.

The shift doesn't begin when life gives it to you.

It begins when your system accepts it ***as already true.***

Your outer reality is not random.
It is a mirror of your internal structure.

Not your thoughts alone but your dominant emotional tone, your subconscious patterns, and the frequency your nervous system maintains.

This is not philosophy. It's function.
Everything you consistently feel, believe, and expect becomes the signal you transmit.
And that signal determines what the field reflects back.

The world doesn't just show you what you want. It shows you what you are.

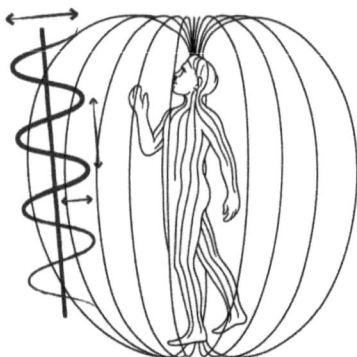

The field operates like a feedback system.
What you hold within, it multiplies outside of you.

If your inner state is chaotic, the field reinforces instability. If your emotional baseline is doubt, the field reflects resistance.

But when your inner environment is coherent, when thought, emotion, and expectation align, the field responds with precision.

It organizes around the version of you that feels most real to your system.
And the version you embody the longest becomes the version life reflects.

This is why internal work is not optional.

You don't get what you visualize.

You get what your nervous system accepts as normal.

Until your subconscious updates its reference point, your results will default to the past.
You may set goals, shift actions, or change environments but without a new internal frequency, the pattern returns.

Change that isn't installed internally can't hold externally.

The field always reads the deeper signal.

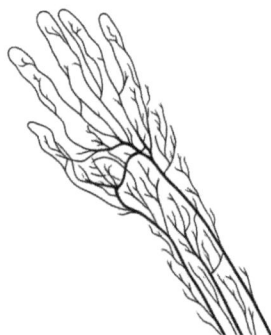

(You are not separate from nature. You are built from it. Your nerves fire like lightning. Your blood flows like rivers. Your breath moves like the wind. As within, so without).

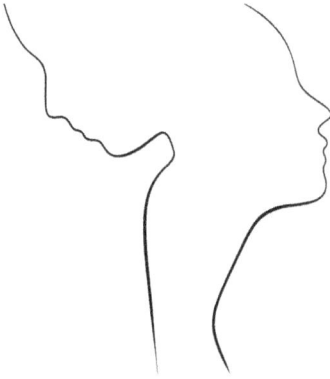

This is where many people fall into contradiction. They chase the external without altering the internal.

They try to force new outcomes while still vibrating old identity.

But the field doesn't respond to contradiction. It responds to coherence.

Until you become the version of you that already has what you want, you'll continue seeing experiences that match the version you haven't yet released.

High performers don't just act differently. They operate from a different internal standard.

They've trained their system to stabilize in the frequency of success.

Not by chance but by emotional consistency, belief conditioning, and subconscious reprogramming.

Their certainty isn't false confidence. It's a signal that has been installed and reinforced until the field had no choice but to comply.

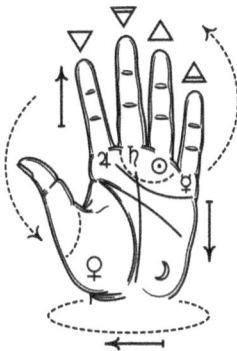

(A geometric pattern showing how frequency builds outward through repeating cycles, structure formed by consistent signal).

(This diagram reflects a deeper truth: the laws of the universe are not outside you, they are mapped within you. You don't follow the cosmos. You are its expression).

The formula is not hidden.
Your internal state is your origin point.
Every thought, emotion, and pattern you sustain becomes part of the signal.
And that signal sculpts your outer reality.

This is the law.
Not moral law, universal law.

What you send is what you meet.
What you embody is what you attract.
What you stabilize becomes your environment.

The question is no longer "Will it work?"
The question is "Can I hold the signal long enough for it to return?"

REFLECTIVE REALITY

Reality doesn't respond to surface change.
It responds to internal structure.

You're not reacting to the world.

You're projecting into it.

Every thought sustained, every emotion repeated, **becomes a broadcast.**

And that broadcast sets the tone for what life reflects.

Change doesn't begin outside.

It begins in signal.

As within, so without.

AS WITHIN, SO WITHOUT

THE UNIVERSE IS WITHIN YOU.

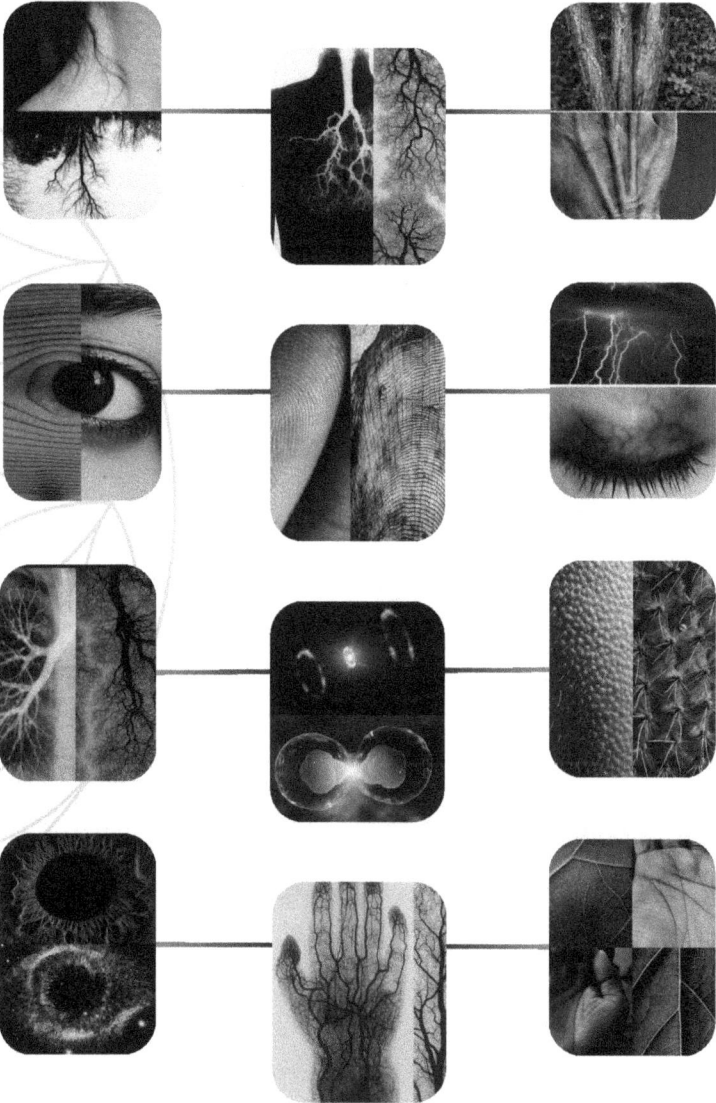

AS WITHIN, SO WITHOUT

THE UNIVERSE IS WITHIN YOU.

You are not observing the universe from outside. You are interfacing with it from within. Your body is not separate from the cosmos. It reflects the same structure and laws that shape stars, atoms, and galaxies.

The field around you is not reacting to reality. It is part of it. From your heart's rhythm to your DNA's coils to your nervous system's branches, you are a microcosmic mirror of the universe.

This is fractal design. A pattern that repeats at every scale. And you are a living expression of it. Consciousness doesn't live in your brain. It radiates through your field. That field is entangled with the fabric of space. It doesn't wait for change. It initiates it.

When you hold a frequency, the field organizes around it. This isn't hope. It's function. You're not separate from the universe. You are its local interface. "As within, so without" was never philosophy. It was observation.

What you hold inside becomes reflected outside because the systems are not separate. They are synchronized. You don't influence reality from the outside. You do it by stabilizing your internal state, because your state is the instruction.

You are not in the universe. You are the universe in a particular form broadcasting back to itself. When this becomes real to you, you stop reaching and you start recalibrating.

FIELD INTEGRITY TEST

Read your Field Imprint Card.

Say it.
Feel it.

Now check
- What part of your body agrees?
- What part pulls away?

You're looking for signal friction. Not fixing, just noticing.

Find the Break Point

What makes the signal drop?
- A specific thought?
- A feeling of doubt?
- Waiting for proof?

Write one line:
The signal breaks when:

Go Back To Your Imprint.

Stand in it.
Let your system get used to it.

"I'm not here to chase proof.
I'm here to hold signal.
The field follows consistency."

SECTION II: FREQUENCY MECHANICS

Thought is not passive. It is the initial structure of reality: an internal signal that, once held with enough emotional charge and repetition, begins to shape the external world.

Most people assume thoughts float meaninglessly through the mind. But in reality, each thought is a blueprint. A design. A structural instruction. It is the precursor to energy movement. And energy movement is what reality listens to.

The field does not wait for intention. It responds to instruction, and thought is the first layer of that instruction.

$$(a + b) / a = a / b = \varphi \approx 1.618$$

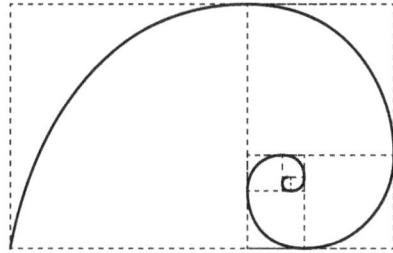

(The Golden Ratio is a mathematical pattern showing how structure and consistency form natural order).

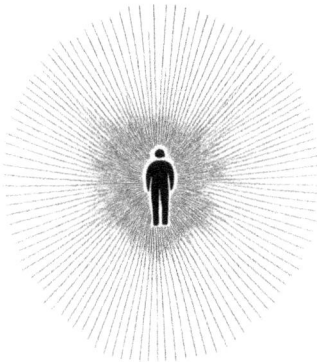

The form of a thought matters less than the feeling it rides on. A calm thought has different consequences than an urgent one, even if the words are identical.

You can say "I'm ready for change" while still transmitting resistance. That resistance carries a different frequency. And the field will respond more directly to that frequency than to your spoken or internal language.

Thought becomes form not because of what it says, but because of what it sends.

Every thought emits a code. The emotion behind it determines whether that code is scrambled or clear.

This is why passing thoughts don't always create change. Sustained ones do.

When a thought is focused on long enough, with emotion present, it begins to affect posture, perception, and behavior. That creates feedback loops. Your body changes, your decisions shift, and new data emerges to reinforce the original signal.
Now, the shift becomes visible.

This is form in motion. It is not random. It is pattern-based. What was once intangible becomes structural.

And the more often the loop completes, the more deeply the new form embeds into your identity.

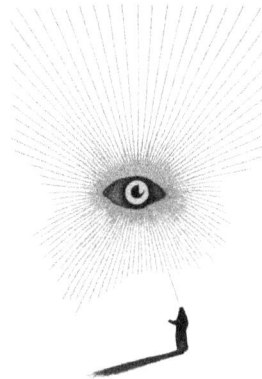

The more coherent the thought-emotion pair, the more quickly it takes shape. Fragmented signals create delays. But focused thought, paired with a steady emotional baseline, creates instruction the field can immediately begin to organize around.

This is not about force. It is about precision. When a thought is held with energetic integrity, it becomes a command. The clearer the command, the faster reality conforms.

Thought without coherence stays theoretical. But thought backed by emotion becomes executable by the system.

This is the real origin of "manifestation."

It is not belief without effort. It is structured instruction through thought. The thought tells the nervous system what to expect. The nervous system broadcasts that expectation through emotion. That emotion modifies the electromagnetic field. And the field begins attracting or repelling accordingly.

Reality bends not to desire, but to instruction. When people say "it just happened," what they don't realize is that the instruction had already been installed, often long before the result appeared.

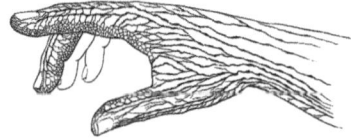

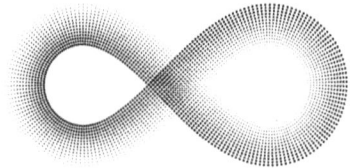

To change form, you begin with structure. And structure begins with thought. But it must be a thought you can hold. Not mentally, but energetically. A thought backed by alignment, emotional, somatic, and subconscious.

Without that alignment, thought stays theoretical. But once the system begins to believe it, the field listens. And when the field listens, form begins.

There is no bypassing this sequence.

Reality cannot exceed the coherence of the signal that shaped it.

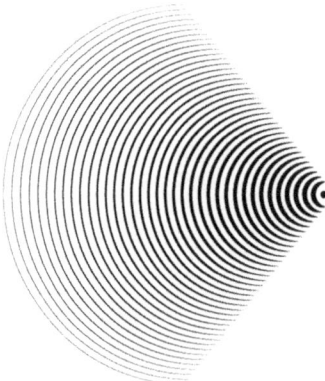

THOUGHT INTO FORM

Thought isn't passive,
it's your active
blueprint for reality.

It imprints the field,
the field shapes
experience.

Consistency creates
structure.

Fragmentation
weakens the form.

This isn't philosophy,
it's physics.

Every thought
repeated enough,
crystallizes into form.

Thought mastery
means sustaining
clarity,

so reality mirrors
intention, effortlessly.

Every thought you think travels through a filter. That filter is belief. It determines whether the signal is accepted, rejected, or distorted before it ever reaches the subconscious.

A belief isn't just a thought you keep thinking. It's a frequency your nervous system has accepted as true. And once accepted, it operates automatically, shaping perception, behavior, and outcomes without conscious input.

Why beliefs are powerful: They don't just influence your thoughts. They filter your reality. You literally cannot see evidence that contradicts a deeply held belief. Your brain filters it out before it reaches conscious awareness.

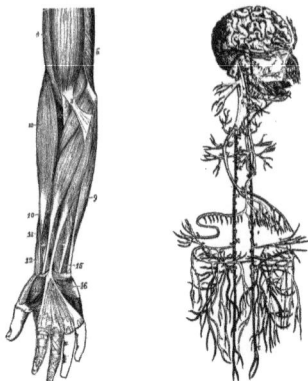

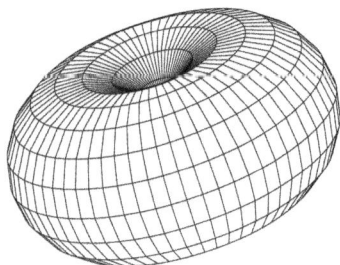

Most beliefs were installed before you had language. Before age seven, your brain operates in theta state, a hypnotic frequency where information bypasses critical thinking and goes straight into the subconscious.

Every repeated message, every emotional charge, every pattern you witnessed became encoded. Not as memory, but as the operating system. These beliefs now run in the background, determining what feels possible, safe, or true.

You don't question them because they feel like reality itself. But they're not reality. They're just the lens you've been looking through. Change the lens, and reality reorganizes.

A belief becomes a self-fulfilling prophecy. If you believe success requires struggle, you'll unconsciously create struggle to validate the belief. The field doesn't judge your beliefs. It just matches them. Whatever you accept internally becomes mirrored externally. This is why two people in the same circumstances can have completely different outcomes. Different beliefs, different filters, different realities.

From quantum physics: The observer effect proves this. The act of observation collapses the wave function. But what determines how it collapses? The observer's expectation. Your belief is your expectation. And your expectation determines which version of reality you experience.

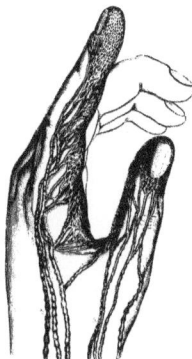

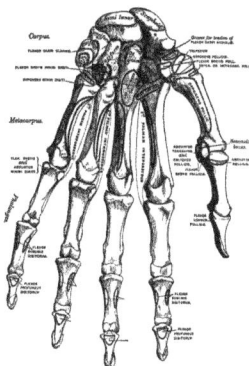

Most people try to change their results without changing their beliefs. They work harder, try new strategies, push through resistance. But if the underlying belief hasn't shifted, the pattern stays the same.

You can't outwork a belief. You can only reprogram it. And reprogramming happens through emotional repetition, not intellectual understanding.

The mechanism: Your subconscious doesn't respond to logic. It responds to feeling. When you pair a new thought with sustained emotion, the subconscious begins to treat it as real. The belief shifts. And when the belief shifts, behavior changes automatically.

This is why affirmations fail for most people. They repeat words without feeling. The subconscious hears the words but feels the doubt underneath. And the doubt is the stronger signal.

What actually works: Feel the new belief as if it's already true. Not "I will be successful." But "Success is my natural state." And then find evidence, however small, that supports it. Your brain will start looking for more. Then the filter begins to shift.

The more you reinforce the new belief with emotion and evidence, the faster it installs. And once installed, it becomes your new baseline. What once felt impossible now feels inevitable.

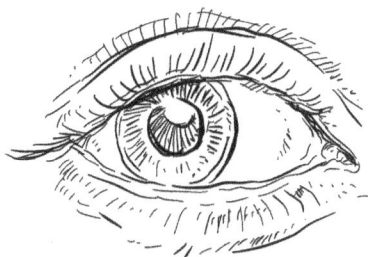

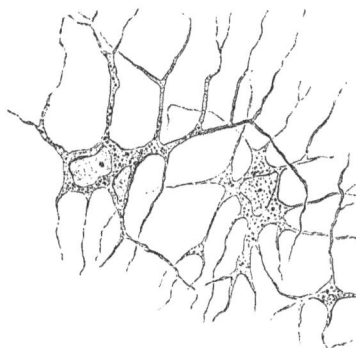

The belief layer is the foundation. Thought may be the blueprint, but belief determines which blueprints get built.

If your beliefs don't support your vision, your vision stays theoretical.

But when belief and thought align, the field has no choice but to comply. The signal is clear. The instruction is consistent. And form begins to take shape, not through force, but through resonance.

Stop trying to believe. Start choosing what you accept as true. Then live from that truth until your nervous system catches up. That's how you rewrite the code.

THE BELIEF LAYER

Belief is the filter between thought and form.

It determines what gets through, what gets distorted, what gets blocked.

Beliefs aren't truth. They're agreements.

And any agreement can be rewritten.

When you shift the belief, the signal clarifies.

When the signal clarifies, reality reorganizes.

This isn't positive thinking.

It's structural reprogramming.

THE BELIEF LAYER

ANCHOR YOUR CORE BELIEF. BROADCAST ITS EFFECT.

Describe your core belief clearly:

- *What empowering belief are you living by right now?*

....

....

....

....

- *What thoughts and convictions reinforce this belief?*

....

....

....

....

Example prompts:
- *I believe in my limitless capacity to create and grow.*
- *I trust that every challenge is a step toward my success.*
- *My beliefs align perfectly with the reality I want to build.*
- *I am worthy of abundance and positive transformation.*

Your signal is always broadcasting. But not all broadcasts are clean.

Signal interference happens when your conscious intention conflicts with your subconscious programming.

You say you want success, but your body broadcasts doubt. You visualize abundance, but your nervous system is locked in survival mode.

The field doesn't respond to your words. It responds to your dominant frequency. And when that frequency is contradictory, the signal fragments. Results become inconsistent. Outcomes feel random. But they're not random. They're responding to a mixed message.

Most interference comes from unresolved emotion. And until you identify them, they'll keep scrambling your signal.

You can have perfect strategy, clear vision, and disciplined action. But if your emotional frequency is broadcasting lack, fear, or unworthiness, those emotions will override everything else.

Your amygdala scans for threat 24/7. When it detects danger, real or imagined, it hijacks your nervous system. Cortisol floods your body. Your heart rate spikes. Your field contracts. No matter what you're consciously thinking, your body is broadcasting "survival." And the field responds accordingly.

This is why trying harder doesn't always work.

When your "effort" is driven by fear, the dominant signal isn't the action. It's the emotion behind it.

Action powered by lack creates more lack. Intentions backed by emotional contradiction collapse under their own weight.

The field doesn't respond to your words. It responds to the emotional instructions your nervous system believes.

And the most consistent frequency, not the most urgent, becomes the default.

(Athena represents strategic clarity, the alignment of thought and action without emotional contradiction).

You may already be sending these mixed messages without knowing it. The urge to prove yourself. The need to control outcomes. The habit of over-explaining. These aren't surface behaviors. They're embedded instructions. And unless they're seen, they won't stop.

And the longer the contradiction goes unchecked, the more it becomes your baseline.

What to look for: Notice where you feel tension when you think about your goal. That's interference. Notice where you're explaining, justifying, or defending. That's interference. Each one is a flag showing you where your frequency is contradictory.

Signal conflict isn't a flaw. It's a result of layered programming. Most of what creates interference was installed before you had conscious choice. Childhood patterns. Cultural conditioning. Survival mechanisms that once protected you but now limit you.

But now that you understand how it works, you can begin isolating it.
Not by fighting it, but by recognizing it.

When you spot the contradiction, the awareness itself begins to dissolve the pattern. You're no longer unconsciously broadcasting mixed messages. You're consciously choosing which signal to amplify.

This is where calibration begins. Not by pushing harder, but by aligning cleaner.

Most people try to force their way through interference. They add more effort, more action, more intensity. But that just amplifies the contradiction.

The next chapter will show you how to do that, not by amplifying your emotion, but by stabilizing your signal. Because when clarity meets consistency, the field has no choice but to reflect it. The interference drops. The static clears. And for the first time, your reality begins responding to your actual intention, not your hidden contradictions.

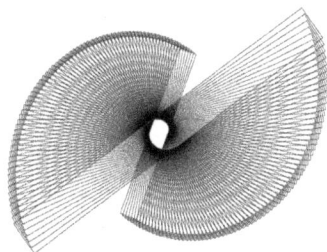

SIGNAL INTERFERENCE

Interference isn't external noise,
it's internal misalignment.

Inconsistent focus scatters intention, weakening manifestation.

Stability sharpens your frequency.

Instability disperses potential.

This goes beyond theory,
it's measurable coherence.

Your clarity directly influences outcomes.

Signal mastery requires focused precision,

so reality can accurately mirror your intent.

Frequency calibration is the process of tuning your frequency until it becomes a steady, coherent broadcast.
Not by controlling every emotion, but by learning how to return to center when you drift.

Most people don't realize they're constantly recalibrating based on external feedback. Someone doubts them, they doubt themselves. An opportunity appears, they get excited, then anxious. The signal shifts with every input. That's reactive calibration.

What you need is active calibration, where you set the frequency and hold it regardless of what's happening around you.

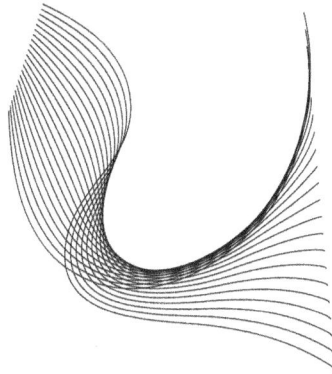

You can tell when your frequency is clear. Your breath slows. Your posture opens. Your speech becomes precise, not rushed. There is no inner wobble. The body becomes congruent with the mind.

This isn't confidence. It's coherence.
You're no longer broadcasting multiple messages. You are sending one. And the field begins listening differently when that clarity is present.

Think of coherent light versus incoherent light. Incoherent light, like a light bulb, scatters in all directions. Weak. Diffuse. Coherent light, like a laser, focuses all photons in the same direction.

Your frequency works the same way.

Your emotional baseline is the anchor of your frequency. Most people's baseline is borrowed. It's inherited from their environment, their upbringing, their culture. They've never consciously chosen it.

Calibration means choosing your baseline.

Identify the emotional state you want as your baseline. Calm? Certain? Focused? Then practice returning to it throughout the day. Not once. Not when you meditate. Every time you notice you've drifted. That's calibration. Most people practice their anxiety 50 times a day and wonder why they're anxious. Practice your chosen baseline 50 times a day instead.

(Your torso is the energetic center of your torus field, the point where internal frequency radiates outward and external input cycles back in).

A calibrated frequency doesn't hinge on outcomes. It's rooted in internal steadiness, a decision held long enough that reality begins to recognize it.

This isn't about needing proof. It's about becoming the proof. And when your signal holds firm under pressure, you stop adjusting to the world. The world begins adjusting to you.

You don't calibrate by trying to feel good. You calibrate by becoming internally steady. You shift from emotional impulse to emotional command. From hoping it works, to moving as if it already is.

The field does not respond to emotion alone. It responds to emotional authority.
When you shift from reacting to selecting your state, you begin controlling the broadcast. And when you control the broadcast, reality reshapes around it.

What this looks like: Someone criticizes you. Old pattern: defense, justification, emotional spike.

Calibrated response: pause, breathe, return to baseline. No reaction. No explanation. Just steady frequency. The criticism lands in empty space because you're not broadcasting the matching frequency to catch it.

(This tarot card (Strength) symbolizes inner mastery, steadying your emotions to lead with calm authority instead of reaction).

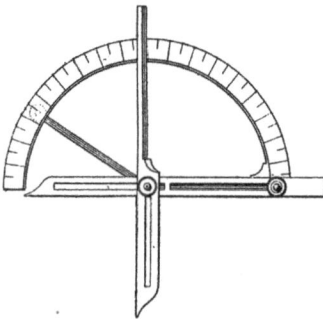

Calibration is a skill. Like any skill, it strengthens with repetition.
At first, you may slip back into loops. But every return to center rewires the system. You start to build emotional muscle. And eventually, holding a steady frequency becomes natural.

It stops being a technique. It becomes who you are. And the field will begin responding in kind, not just occasionally, but reliably.
Most people give up after a few days. They don't feel different, so they assume it's not working. But frequency calibration works like strength training. You don't see muscle after one workout. The adaptation is happening beneath the surface.

FREQUENCY CALIBRATION

Calibration isn't
suppressing emotions,
it's tuning them.

Clear emotions
broadcast clear signals.

Chaotic feelings disrupt
your frequency.

Steady emotion
strengthens
coherence.

Unregulated states blur
the transmission.

Reality matches your
dominant emotional
state.

Frequency calibration
means tuning emotions
deliberately,

so experience reflects
intent, not chance.

Every emotion you feel shapes your frequency.

Some get trapped in cycles, patterns that repeat not because of what's happening now, but because of what was never resolved then.

These are emotional loops. They're like grooves in the nervous system where old reactions keep firing, long after the moment has passed. You might feel like you're responding to the present, but your frequency is still broadcasting from a past imprint. And that distorted signal keeps informing your experience until the loop is broken.

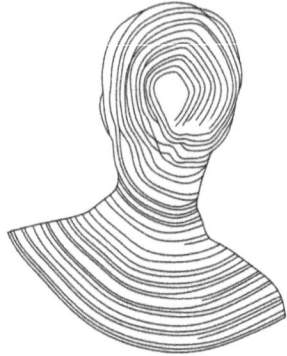

Loops form through emotional repetition. A situation triggers a reaction, the system tenses, and that state gets rehearsed. Over time, the body begins to expect the emotion.

And because it's familiar, it keeps showing up, not just internally, but externally. The loop becomes a filter. You begin attracting experiences that validate the unresolved frequency.

Your nervous system is designed for efficiency. Once a response pattern is established, it becomes automatic. This saved energy for our ancestors. But now it keeps you locked in outdated reactions. The body defaults to what it knows, even when what it knows no longer serves you.

(The Devil doesn't signify evil; it signifies unseen entrapment: emotional addiction, repeated cycles, and the illusion of powerlessness).

You can't resolve a loop with logic.
You have to shift the frequency.
That starts with recognition. Not overanalyzing, just noticing the emotion as it surfaces, and holding presence with it instead of reacting. You breathe. You stay open. You move from reflex to awareness.

Each time you do this, you send a new signal, one that tells the nervous system it's safe to exit the loop.

The practice: When the loop triggers, pause. Name the emotion. "This is anxiety." Don't judge it. Don't try to fix it. Just observe it. That observation creates space. And in that space, the automatic response loses its grip. You're no longer the emotion. You're the awareness watching it.

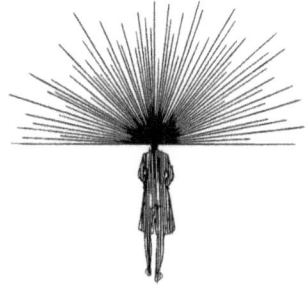

(Fear isn't always danger. Often, it's the body's response to what the mind hasn't named. Lack of awareness creates uncertainty, and uncertainty breeds fear).

Loops often resurface during stress or uncertainty.

When life doesn't go your way, pay attention to what emotion arises first.

Is it panic? Control? Withdrawal?

That's the frequency the loop has trained your body to default to.
But you don't have to obey it

You can shift it in real time, not by fighting it, but by interrupting its momentum.
The key is catching the loop before it completes.

Most people don't notice the emotion until they're already deep inside the reaction.
By then, the body has flooded with hormones, the nervous system has locked into the pattern, and the loop reinforces itself.
But there's a window. A split second between trigger and response.

That's where freedom lives. In that pause, you can choose differently. Not by suppressing the emotion, but by witnessing it without becoming it.

Every time you break the loop, you're weakening the old neural pathway and strengthening a new one. After 30-60 repetitions, the new response becomes the default.

(Like Ganymedes feeding the eagle, you consciously nurture the force that lifts you above old habits. Each deliberate choice strengthens your frequency).

Breaking a loop isn't about perfection. You'll slip. You'll catch yourself halfway through the old reaction and think you failed. You didn't. Catching yourself halfway is progress. Next time you'll catch it sooner.

This is how reprogramming actually works. Not through force. Through iteration. Each time you interrupt the pattern, even partially, you're building new neural architecture. The old pathway doesn't disappear immediately. It fades with disuse. And the new pathway strengthens with repetition.

Eventually, the old emotional response stops feeling like "you." It starts feeling foreign. That's when you know the loop is breaking.

THE EMOTION TRAP

Emotion isn't fleeting,
it's formative.

*Repeated feelings
solidify into patterns.*

*Unresolved cycles trap
your frequency.*

*Awareness disrupts
emotional loops.*

*Unconscious habits
reinforce limitation.*

***Your dominant
emotions guide reality.***

*Unexamined emotions
maintain unwanted
outcomes.*

*Escaping the emotion
trap means conscious
recalibration,*

***so experience reflects
choice, not
conditioning.***

EMOTIONAL SIGNAL SCAN

OWN YOUR SIGNAL. COMMAND THE FIELD.

Find your most repeated emotional frequency.

Steps

For the next 24 hours, track how you feel after any challenge or discomfort.

Write down the dominant emotion each time.
One word. No journaling.

At the end of the day, look for the pattern.

Ask Is this the signal I want to keep sending?

- -

Write This
If I were broadcasting the signal I actually want to live in, it would feel like:

And This
The state I want my nervous system to recognize as home is:

Your frequency doesn't live in your head.

It lives in how you move.

How you breathe. How you hold yourself when no one's watching.

Embodiment is the point where what you believe internally starts showing up in how you exist physically. Not performing it. Not faking it. Actually becoming it.

When your body mirrors the frequency you're building, the field stops receiving mixed signals. It reads you as one coherent message.

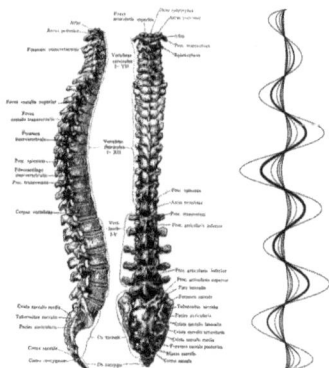

Most people's bodies betray them. They say they're confident, but their shoulders are tight and their breathing is shallow.

They claim they're ready for success, but their posture says they're bracing for failure.

The field doesn't listen to your words. It reads your body. Every microexpression. Every rushed movement. Every time you fidget or avoid eye contact or speak too fast. Your body broadcasts the truth even when your mouth is lying.

And until your body starts moving like the outcome already happened, reality will keep reflecting the frequency your body is actually sending.

There's a difference between wanting something and embodying it.

When you want it, you're reaching. Chasing. Explaining. Justifying.

When you embody it, none of that is necessary. Your nervous system settles.
Your tone changes. You stop needing external validation because internally, the question is already answered.
That shift is magnetic, not because it's louder, but because there's no friction. No contradiction.

People feel it before you speak. And the field responds to it faster than any amount of visualization or affirmation ever could.

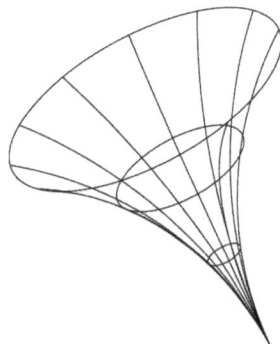

CHAPTER 6: EMBODIED FREQUENCY

You don't force your body to embody a frequency. You rehearse it until it becomes automatic.

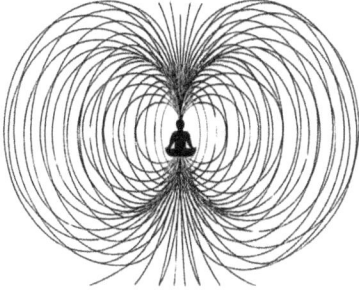

If you want calm, you have to move calmly. Even when chaos is around you, especially then.

If you want certainty, you stop explaining yourself and defending your decisions.

Your body learns through repetition, not theory. Every time you move in alignment with the frequency you're building, your nervous system logs it as evidence. And when the evidence stacks high enough, your body stops resisting.

It accepts the new state as real.

The body is not just matter, it's frequency.

In esoteric and occult systems, the physical form is seen as the communicator between the inner world and the outer one.

The Old High German word for "body" comes from botah, meaning "messenger."

When your internal signal becomes clear, the body delivers it without distortion. But when that signal is unstable, the body reveals it just as clearly.

This is why embodiment is the final test. It shows what your system actually believes, not what you hope it believes.

(The word "body" shares roots with the Old High German "botah", meaning "messenger." In many esoteric systems, the body isn't just seen as matter, it's the messenger of the mind).

When you live in embodied frequency, reality shifts around you.

Doors open without you knocking. Conversations flow without effort. Opportunities appear without you hunting them down.

Not because the universe suddenly likes you. Because your signal is clean. Your body, your words, your energy are all saying the same thing.

There's nothing for the field to filter or interpret. You're not broadcasting potential anymore. You're broadcasting presence. And presence is what reality responds to.

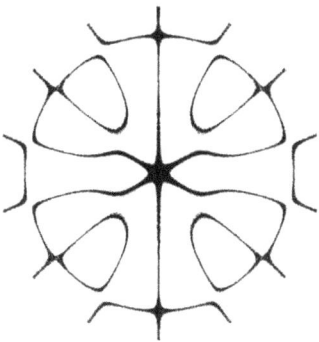

EMBODIED FREQUENCY

*The body isn't passive, **it's your messenger.***

Every posture broadcasts intention.

Movement encodes frequency into form.

Aligned physiology amplifies coherence.

Your physical state imprints reality.

Embodied clarity anchors stable outcomes.

Embodied frequency means intentional presence,

so reality responds clearly to your physical instruction.

Everything in existence vibrates.

Your thoughts. Your emotions. The chair you're sitting on. The book in your hands.
All of it is frequency in motion.

Resonance is what happens when two frequencies match and begin amplifying each other.

This is physics. A tuning fork can make another fork vibrate without touching it. Your internal state does the same thing with reality.

Whatever frequency you hold most consistently starts calling in experiences, people, and circumstances that match it.

Resonance doesn't care what you want.

It cares what you are.

If anxiety is your baseline, you'll keep pulling in situations that validate anxiety. If clarity is your baseline, life starts organizing around that instead.

The field isn't trying to help you or hurt you. It's neutral. It's a mirror.

And it reflects whatever signal you're broadcasting most consistently.
Not the signal you're trying to send.

The one you're actually holding.

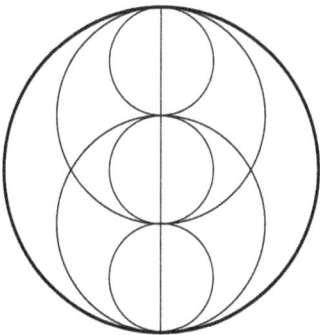

This is why people stay stuck.

They think new thoughts but hold old frequencies.

They visualize success while their body is preparing for disappointment. They say they want change while their energy is screaming familiarity.

The field doesn't respond to wishes. It responds to what's real in your system. And what's real shows up in your baseline emotional state. The frequency you return to when nothing external is demanding your attention.

That's the frequency that shapes your reality.

The more consistent your frequency, the more your environment stabilizes.

Not because you're controlling outcomes. Because you're no longer sending contradictory signals.

Some people seem to attract ease without trying. It's not luck. It's resonance. They've cleaned their signal to the point where struggle doesn't match their frequency anymore.

The field mirrors their consistency. And because their baseline is stable, their reality becomes predictable. Not boring. Aligned.

The law of resonance doesn't reward effort. It rewards state.

And state isn't built with affirmations or vision boards. It's built with your dominant thoughts, your actions, and your daily emotional baseline.

You can't fake resonance.
But you can build it.

You repeat the frequency you want until your system recognizes it as home. And when it becomes home, the external world starts reorganizing to match it.

Not all at once. But inevitably.

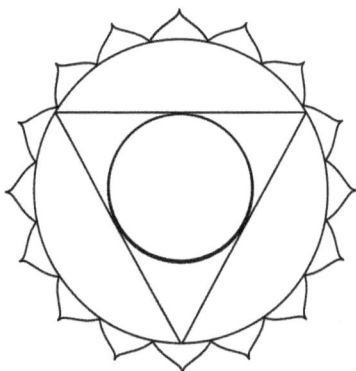

Resonance is exact.

If you're sending out a clear frequency, reality will start harmonizing with it.

If you're scattered, life will mirror that too. This isn't punishment. It's feedback.

Every mismatch shows you where your frequency is off. Every alignment shows you where it's locked in.

Once you understand this, you stop chasing results. You start tuning your signal. And you let the field handle the rest.

THE LAW OF RESONANCE

*Resonance is the law
of attraction*
made tangible.

*Like attracts like in
frequency and form.*

*Coherent vibration
draws aligned
experience.*

*Discordant waves
repel or distort
outcomes.*

*This is not wishful
thinking,*
it's natural law.

*Mastering resonance
means tuning your
core signal,*

**so life responds with
exact harmony.**

THE LAW OF RESONANCE

ANCHOR YOUR FREQUENCY. BROADCAST THE OUTCOME.

Describe your resonant signal clearly:

- *What vibration are you tuning into and sending out right now?*

....

....

....

....

- *What thoughts, feelings, and intentions amplify this resonance?*

....

....

....

....

Example prompts:
- *I attract people and opportunities that match my energy.*
- *My frequency harmonizes with success and growth.*
- *I resonate with clarity, purpose, and abundance.*
- *I am a magnet for aligned experiences and connections.*

CHAPTER 8: ENERGETIC GRAVITY

Some emotional states carry more weight than others. Not metaphorically. Literally.

The more concentrated an emotional frequency becomes, the more it warps the space around you.

This is gravity. Not the kind that holds planets in orbit, but the kind that pulls experiences, people, and circumstances into your field.

The denser your emotional state, the stronger the pull. This is why people locked into scarcity keep encountering scarcity. Their emotional density is concentrated there. Everything begins circling that center point.

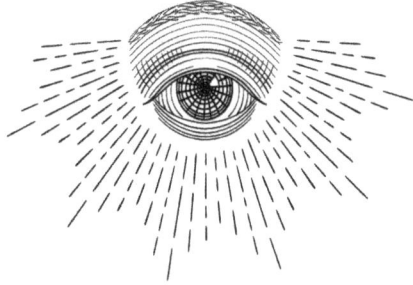

The field doesn't just listen to you. It organizes around you.

Every thought you sustain, every emotion you rehearse, every state you return to adds mass to your signal.

Light frequencies pass through quickly. They don't anchor. But heavy, sustained emotions create gravitational wells. This is why intense fear reshapes reality faster than mild hope. Fear is dense. Hope without conviction is weightless.

The field responds to density, not intention. And density comes from consistency. From holding one frequency long enough that it becomes the heaviest thing in your field.

You've felt this in others.
Some people walk into a space and everything bends toward them. Conversations. Attention. Not because they're demanding it. Because their presence has mass.

Other people try for years and can't get momentum. They're doing all the right things on paper, but nothing sticks.

It's not that they're unlucky. Their energy is diffused. Spread thin across a dozen worries, doubts, and distractions.

They're broadcasting in every direction at once. Scattered energy creates no pull. Concentrated energy becomes inevitable.

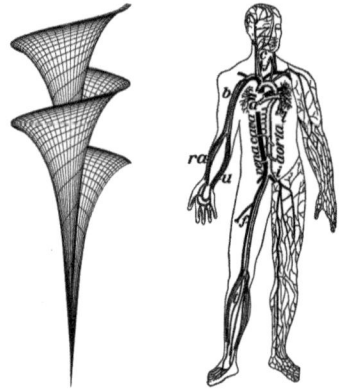

To shift your gravitational field, you need to collapse your focus into one emotional direction. Not five goals. Not three backup plans.

One direction. One signal. One dominant state.

This is what creates a Chief Aim.

Not the goal itself, but the emotional mass you place behind it. When your energy stops leaking into hypotheticals and regrets and "what ifs," it begins to consolidate. And consolidated energy creates force. That force doesn't push outcomes. It draws them. Silently. Steadily. Like gravity itself.

Your nervous system determines the density of your field. When it stabilizes, your broadcast thickens. And the thicker the broadcast, the harder it is for interference to penetrate.

You'll notice it in real time. Chaos that used to hook you now slides past. Drama that used to consume you loses its grip. Not because you're avoiding it. Because your field has become too dense for low-frequency disturbances to affect.

And as your field stabilizes, higher-frequency experiences begin moving into your orbit. Not because you're chasing them. Because the gravitational match became natural.

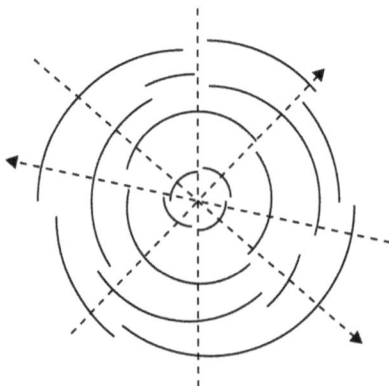

Energetic gravity doesn't announce itself. It doesn't perform. It doesn't need validation. It simply exists at a certain density, and reality reorganizes around it.

When your field reaches that density, you stop pushing. You stop convincing. You stop explaining.

You're not trying to make things happen anymore. You're standing in a center of mass that pulls exactly what matches it. And once that pull becomes your default state, momentum isn't something you generate. It's something that follows you.

ENERGETIC GRAVITY

Energetic gravity
pulls what matches
your core
frequency.

Stable energy
centers attract
aligned experience.

Unsteady fields
repel or create
friction.

This is not theory,
it's natural
consequence.

Mastering energetic
gravity means
strengthening your
core,

so your reality
naturally orbits
your intention.

BRAINWAVES

Your brain emits more than thoughts.

It emits waves, measurable
electromagnetic frequencies that affect
how your body feels and how your field
broadcasts.

Each brainwave state influences the
clarity, strength, and impact of your
signal.

And that signal determines how reality
responds.

In the next pages, we will explore
each wave.

BETA (13–30 HZ)

Function - Waking consciousness, problem-solving, logic

State - Fast, alert, external focus

Emotional tone - Tension, mental effort, vigilance

Field impact - Scattered signal, reduced coherence

How to shift -
- Breathe deeper
- Stop thinking about the past
- Drop back into your body and the present

Most people live here, stuck in noise, sending fragmented signals.

Beta is useful, but not where transformation happens.

ALPHA (8–13 HZ)

Function - Relaxed focus, gateway to the subconscious

State - Present, aware, emotionally neutral

Emotional tone - Calm, receptive, balanced

Field impact - Clearer signal, field begins to stabilize

How to access -
- Close your eyes for 30 seconds
- Focus on breath and body sensations
- Sit in stillness without input

Alpha is where suggestion begins.

Your field becomes more impressionable, and the nervous system softens enough to receive.

THETA (4–8 HZ)

Function - Deep subconscious access, emotional imprinting

State - Hypnosis, meditation, memory reconsolidation

Emotional tone - Surrender, openness, sensitivity

Field impact - Direct subconscious access, malleable reality

How to enter -
- Use audio tracks with binaural beats or solfeggio tones
- Enter trance through slow rhythmic breath
- Visualize calmly with emotion before sleep

Theta is the installation zone. What you feel here, the body believes. What the body believes, the field reinforces.

DELTA (0.5–4 HZ)

Function - Deep unconscious healing. Nervous system recalibration. Cellular regeneration.

State - Dreamless sleep. Pure stillness. Ego dissolved. No identity, no thought.

Emotional tone - Void-like calm. Emptiness without fear.

Field impact - Complete energetic reset. Foundational coherence restored. The field purges old interference.

How to enter -
- Sleep in total darkness and silence
- Use Delta-frequency binaural tones (0.5–4 Hz)
- Release all mental activity, identity, and effort

Delta is not for programming. It's for clearing.

Here, the field resets itself.
Old patterns dissolve without effort, and the system heals in silence.

GAMMA (30–100 HZ+)

Function - Peak coherence, instant integration

State - Expanded awareness, joy, synchronicity

Emotional tone - Euphoria, love, unity

Field impact - High-voltage broadcast, fastest result feedback

How to cultivate -
- Practice gratitude deeply and often
- Visualize while in a heart-coherent state
- Combine intention with elevated emotion until it feels done

Gamma collapses time.

It sends your instruction with maximum precision.

It's the frequency of wholeness, where you stop seeking and start being. This is the state where change becomes immediate, not theoretical.

Energy moves. That's its nature. The question is whether you're directing it or whether it's directing you.

Most people are passengers. Their energy reacts to whatever stimulus appears. A bad email and their energy collapses. A good opportunity and their energy spikes, then crashes when doubt creeps in. They're riding the wave, not steering it.

Energy can be steered. Not through brute force, but through conscious direction. The same way you'd guide water through channels instead of trying to hold it in your hands. Energy follows the path you create for it with your attention.

(The Egyptian Neteru don't symbolize gods; they symbolize internal systems. Thoth is thought, Anubis is death, Horus is vision, Ma'at is law, Osiris is power, and Isis is reconstruction).

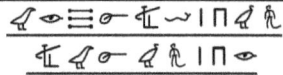

Attention is the first point of control. Because wherever attention goes, energy accumulates.

Most people leak attention constantly. Checking notifications. Replaying arguments. Imagining disasters that haven't happened. Worrying about things they can't control. And their energy follows every leak.

Energy manipulation begins when you reclaim attention. When you stop letting external triggers dictate where your energy flows. When you choose where to place your focus and hold it there long enough for energy to build. Because energy without direction is just noise. Energy with direction becomes force.

(The Eye of Horus truly represented conscious awareness as a tool of energetic and spiritual control, it symbolized the act of seeing not just with the eyes, but with the mind, the will, and the soul).

Once you control attention, you shape energy through three channels: thought, word, and action. These aren't separate. They're stages of the same broadcast.

How you think creates the internal blueprint. How you speak either reinforces that blueprint or fractures it. And how you act either proves the blueprint is real or reveals it as fantasy.

When all three align, your signal becomes coherent. When they contradict, your energy scatters and reality stays unclear.

This is why people who "talk a good game" but don't follow through never manifest. Their words and actions are broadcasting different signals.

(The Ankh is not just a symbol of life, it's a diagram of how energy becomes experience. From intention → through focus → into form).

You've been manipulating energy since you were born. Every emotion you've felt, every thought you've sustained, every decision you've made has bent the field in some direction.

The difference now is awareness. Most people manipulate energy unconsciously. Toward fear when they worry. Toward limitation when they doubt. Toward chaos when they react. They're using the same power, just without precision.

Conscious energy manipulation isn't about learning a new skill. It's about directing the skill you've always had. Toward creation instead of destruction. Toward alignment instead of resistance. Toward what you actually want instead of what you're afraid of.

(TThe Magician symbolizes focused creation, drawing energy from the unseen, aligning it through thought, word, and action, and imprinting it into form).

When thought, word, and action move in the same direction, your energy becomes a laser. Your thinking doesn't spiral into doubt. Your words don't contradict your intentions. Your actions confirm what your system has decided.

And when that alignment becomes consistent, the field stops testing you. It stops throwing obstacles. It starts responding. You become a known pattern.

The more stable your internal pattern becomes, the more the external world begins reflecting it back to you. Not occasionally. Consistently.

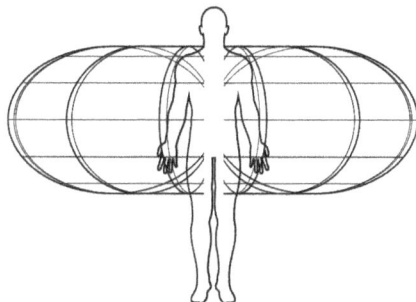

(Field integrity is the foundation of energy manipulation, the clearer and more stable your aura, the more precisely the external world conforms to your internal signal).

Energy manipulation is not mystical. It's mechanical. You're always broadcasting a signal. Always bending the field. Always creating the next moment through what you're holding now.

The only question is whether you're doing it with intention or by default. With clarity or confusion. With alignment or contradiction.

When you start generating from a place of internal coherence instead of external reaction, life doesn't become effortless. But it does become fluid. You're no longer fighting the current.

You're moving with it.

ENERGY MANIPULATION

*Energy is the tool
of **deliberate
creation.***

*Shaping your
internal state
directs external
outcomes.*

*Focused intent
moves **unseen
forces into form.***

*Scatter and
confusion weaken
your influence.*

*This is not
guesswork, it's
applied mastery.*

*Energy
manipulation
means precise
control,*

***so reality
responds exactly
to your will.***

ENERGY MANIPULATION

RECLAIM ATTENTION. SHARPEN BROADCAST.

Set your field direction:

- What are you consciously channeling your energy into right now?

....

....

....

....

- Are your thoughts, words, and actions aligned with that direction?

....

....

....

....

Example prompts:
- *I'm directing energy into building, not reacting.*
- *My focus, speech, and actions are reinforcing the same outcome.*
- *I'm no longer scattering, I move with deliberate current.*
- *My signal is clean, and the field is beginning to reflect that clarity.*

SECTION III: EXTERNAL NAVIGATION

Your field arrives before you do.
Before you speak, before you gesture, before you even enter a room, your electromagnetic presence is already there, establishing tone and setting the baseline frequency of the space.

People don't consciously recognize it, but they feel it at a subconscious level. Some individuals shift the energy of a room the moment they walk in because their field is coherent, dense, and organized. Others enter without creating any shift at all because their field is scattered, reactive, trying to match the environment instead of setting it.

This isn't about charisma or personality.
It's about field coherence and the clarity of your electromagnetic broadcast.

(The Caduceus represents the body's energetic system, two opposing forces moving through the spine to regulate balance and internal order. It directs the inner flow; the torus field moves it outward).

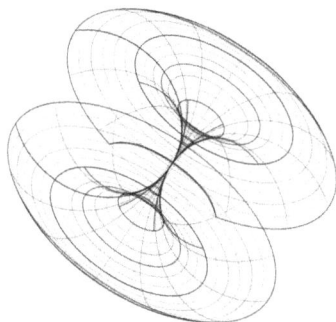

Field dynamics operate on the principle of resonance, not force. A strong field doesn't push, demand, or dominate the space around it. It simply holds its frequency so steadily that other frequencies begin orienting toward it, similar to how a tuning fork causes nearby instruments to resonate at the same pitch.

This is coherence creating alignment, not control creating compliance.

The field that remains most stable becomes the reference point that everything else adjusts to. When your internal state is fragmented, your field broadcasts mixed signals and the environment remains unaffected. When your internal state is unified, your field becomes magnetic and the space reorganizes around you.

Your field operates as a radius of influence, and within that radius, other electromagnetic fields respond in one of three ways.

They either align with your frequency, creating resonance and mutual amplification. They resist it, creating friction and energetic pushback. Or they remain neutral, neither harmonizing nor opposing, simply coexisting without significant interaction.

Most people move through life generating neutral responses because their field isn't broadcasting clearly enough to cause any measurable shift. Their signal is too weak, too inconsistent, or too fragmented to register as a coherent frequency that demands response.

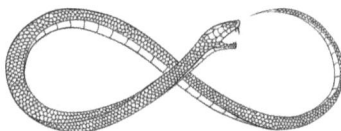

(You generate reality, and reality regenerates you. The loop never breaks. Only your awareness of it changes).

When your field stabilizes and your internal coherence reaches a certain threshold, external reality begins responding in noticeable ways.

Doors that were previously closed start opening without obvious explanation. Conversations shift in your favor even when you're not actively trying to influence them. Opportunities appear that weren't visible before, not because they didn't exist, but because your field has become dense enough to interact with those probability streams.

This isn't attraction through thought or visualization. It's your electromagnetic field becoming coherent enough to reorganize the probability field around you.

(The mirror doesn't smile until you do).

This is mechanics, not metaphysics or spiritual theory. Your field is always interacting with other fields, always exchanging information with the electromagnetic environment around you.
Every person, object, and space you encounter has its own field, and those fields are constantly influencing each other through resonance, interference, and entrainment. The question isn't whether these interactions are happening. They are, continuously, whether you're aware of them or not. The real question is whether you're consciously shaping those interactions through deliberate field management, or whether you're being unconsciously shaped by the dominant fields around you.

Most people are passengers in their own field dynamics, allowing external frequencies to determine their internal state rather than establishing an internal frequency strong enough to influence external conditions.

They walk into a tense room and become tense. They encounter chaos and become chaotic. Their field is reactive rather than generative, responsive rather than directive.

But when you understand field dynamics and train your coherence deliberately, you stop being shaped by every environment you enter. Instead, you become the stabilizing force. Your field sets the tone. And reality begins organizing around the frequency you're holding.

(Anubis was the god who weighed the heart against the feather in the Hall of Ma'at. If the heart was heavy with distortion (fear, contradiction, deceit), the soul couldn't move forward).

FIELD DYNAMICS

Your field is the interface **between you and reality.**

Its strength shapes the flow of energy and events.

Coherent fields draw opportunity and alignment.

Fragmented fields invite resistance and chaos.

This is not speculation, **it's measurable influence.**

Mastering field dynamics means maintaining integrity,

so your environment moves in sync with your intent.

Reality functions as a readback system, reflecting back the actual frequency you're emitting rather than the frequency you think you're broadcasting. Most people have a significant gap between their conscious intention and their actual electromagnetic output.

The field doesn't care about your thoughts or your affirmations. It responds to your actual state, the frequency encoded in your body's electromagnetic output. This is why people can think positive thoughts for years and see no change in their external circumstances - they're broadcasting one frequency while believing they're broadcasting another.

(Hermes represents the neutral return of what is sent, the living principle behind the Hermetic law "As within, so without," where the outer world reflects the inner with exacting precision).

If you believe you're aligned with abundance, but you check your bank account multiple times a day and flinch at prices, then you are making decisions from scarcity.

Reality reads the truth beneath your conscious thoughts, not the story you tell yourself about what you believe or who you are.

Your electromagnetic field is generated by your nervous system's actual state, not by the mental narrative running through your mind. This is the gap that keeps most people stuck - they're working on the wrong level, trying to change outcomes by changing thoughts when reality responds to frequency.

This is why the same patterns keep appearing in your life, often with frustrating consistency. Reality isn't punishing you, being unfair, or working against you. It's showing you, with mechanical precision, the frequency you're actually holding beneath your conscious awareness.

If you keep experiencing financial struggle, your field is broadcasting scarcity regardless of what you consciously think about money.

The external is always a precise mirror of your actual internal frequency, not your aspirational one.

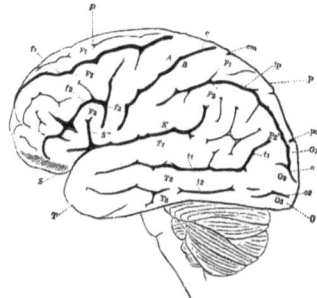

(The Reticular Activating System filters reality to match your dominant focus, it lets through what aligns with your internal settings and ignores what doesn't).

The feedback loop operates with mechanical consistency: your internal state generates an electromagnetic frequency, that frequency broadcasts into the field around you, the field responds by organizing external circumstances that match that frequency, and those circumstances then reinforce your internal state.

This creates a self-perpetuating cycle that becomes increasingly difficult to break the longer it runs. When you're in a positive loop, your good state creates good outcomes which reinforce your good state. When you're in a negative loop, your difficult state creates difficult outcomes which reinforce your difficult state. The loop isn't moral or judgmental. It simply amplifies whatever frequency is running.

(The Scale of Ma'at doesn't punish or praise, it reflects the weight of your frequency with perfect neutrality).

Most people try to change their reality by changing their thoughts, using techniques like visualization, affirmation, and intention-setting.

They think about what they want, they imagine having it, they declare it verbally, but nothing in their external circumstances shifts. This happens because reality doesn't respond to thoughts, it responds to frequency. Your thoughts exist at the mental level, but frequency is generated at the nervous system level, encoded in your body's actual state. You can visualize confidence while your nervous system runs fear patterns.

Thoughts are surface level. Frequency is foundational. Reality reads what's foundational.

(The Phoenix doesn't rise by force, it transforms by releasing what no longer matches its next form).

Breaking the feedback loop requires interrupting it at the actual source, which is your body's held frequency, not your mind's preferred thoughts.

You have to stabilize a genuinely different frequency at the nervous system level, hold it with enough consistency that it becomes your new baseline, and give reality enough time to reorganize in response to that new signal.

This isn't fast and it isn't about feeling good temporarily, it's about creating such sustained coherence in your new frequency that your body accepts it as the new normal. That's when the loop shifts direction because the source frequency has fundamentally changed.

REALITY FEEDBACK LOOPS

*Reality feedback
loops reinforce your*
core frequency.

*The signals you
send shape the
results you get.*

*Consistent input
builds predictable,
aligned outcomes.*

*Disrupted loops
breed chaos,
confusion, and delay.*

This is
cause and effect.

*Master your
feedback loops by
controlling what you
feed in,*

**so your experience
evolves exactly as
you intend.**

REALITY FEEDBACK LOOPS

ANCHOR YOUR FREQUENCY. BROADCAST THE OUTCOME.

Describe your feedback loop clearly:

- *What patterns are you creating through your thoughts and actions?*

....

....

....

....

  - *What thoughts, feelings, and behaviors maintain this loop?*

....

....

....

....

Example prompts:
- *I reinforce habits that propel me toward success.*
- *My actions consistently align with my highest goals.*
- *I break old cycles and build new, empowering ones.*
- *Each day, my reality reflects my deliberate input.*

Energy doesn't disappear or vanish, it redirects and flows toward whatever captures your attention or emotional investment.

Most people hemorrhage energy throughout the day without recognizing where it's going or why their efforts feel ineffective despite working hard.

Every unresolved conversation still cycling through your mind is a leak. Every resentment you're carrying from months or years ago is a leak. Every obligation you agreed to out of guilt rather than genuine alignment is a leak. Every time you say yes when you mean no, energy leaves your system. Every time you hold back truth to keep peace, energy drains. These aren't small losses - they're continuous streams of power flowing away from your field.

(The amphora represents your system's capacity to hold and direct energy, when cracked, intention leaks and momentum disperses).

Your field has a finite amount of energy available at any given moment, and when that energy is scattered across twelve different directions, none of those directions receive enough concentrated power to generate momentum or create tangible results.

You're not weak, incapable, or broken - you're diffused. Your energy is spread so thin across so many incomplete loops and misaligned commitments that no single direction has enough power behind it to produce outcomes. This is why people can work extremely hard and still feel like they're getting nowhere. Diffused energy creates diffused results no matter how much total energy you're expending.

(The Heqa and Nekhakha represent energetic self-mastery, the crook gathers scattered force, the flail refines it into focused direction).

Think carefully about where your attention actually goes throughout a typical day, because attention is the primary mechanism of energy flow.

Every emotional reaction you indulge without awareness drains more from the system than you realize. Energy follows observation. Whatever you repeatedly observe, whether it's anxiety, comparison, or external noise, receives your charge and begins to shape your baseline.

The nervous system doesn't distinguish between meaningful focus and distraction; it only registers activation. The more often you activate unnecessary inputs, the more fragmented your field becomes.

(An alchemical vessel holds energy under pressure, not to suppress it, but to refine it into power).

Your system is built to operate like a closed electrical circuit, efficient, directed, and self-sustaining. But unresolved emotion, distraction, and self-betrayal act like exposed wires bleeding current into empty space.

This is why exhaustion shows up even when you've technically done nothing. It's not the volume of activity; it's the number of open circuits you're unconsciously maintaining.

Until those circuits are closed through completion, release, or alignment, your field keeps compensating for energy that's never returning.

(The cobra above the brow represents the seat of conscious vigilance, awareness that responds with precision, not impulse).

Reclaiming that energy doesn't require dramatic life changes. It requires closure.

Closure means finishing what you start, saying what needs to be said, and letting go of what's not coming back.

Every completion restores integrity to the system. It frees processing power. The field strengthens not through force, but through efficiency, by removing static, not adding effort.

When your internal current stops leaking, even small actions carry exponential impact because all available energy is moving in one direction.

(Aquarius, the water bearer, channels truth into form, directing energy without attachment, distortion, or depletion).

Energetic hygiene is maintenance, not repair. The goal isn't to eliminate every possible drain, but to live with awareness of where energy is being exchanged and to keep that exchange clean.

You'll know when it's clean because the body feels lighter, decisions come faster, and emotion stops looping. Coherence naturally follows conservation.

When energy stops leaking through distraction, resentment, and self-avoidance, the field becomes dense, precise, and directive again. You stop leaking life force into noise and start transmitting signal.

(Like the genie's lamp, energy builds power when contained, only focused release turns potential into creation).

ENERGETIC LEAKAGE

Energetic leakage
drains your core
frequency.

Unfocused energy
scatters your power
and intent.

Small losses
multiply,
weakening your
field.

This isn't vague,
it's measurable
depletion.

Stopping leakage
means tightening
your internal flow,

so every ounce of
energy fuels your
reality with
precision.

Relationships don't just reflect your frequency. They lock it in place.

When you enter a relationship, you establish a frequency contract. Both people agree, usually unconsciously, to maintain certain patterns, roles, and emotional dynamics.

That contract becomes a stabilizing force. Even if you want to change your frequency, the relationship will resist because it's organized around the old one.

This is why personal growth often creates relationship tension. You're trying to change the frequency, but the contract is designed to maintain it.

(Clio is the Muse of History in Greek tradition, tasked with preserving the record of events and proclaiming the truths of the past).

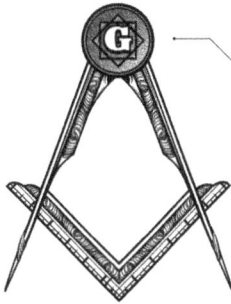

(G = Gnosis, and/or the generative force of reality - God / geometry).

(The compass and square truly represent the conscious construction of reality, precision, alignment, and structure used to shape the unseen into form).

Every long-term relationship has an established resonance pattern. You know exactly how fights will go before they start. You can predict emotional reactions with surprising accuracy. You fall into the same roles repeatedly.

This isn't about personality. It's about frequency synchronization. Your fields have entrained to each other, creating a joint frequency that both people maintain unconsciously.

Breaking that pattern requires both people changing simultaneously, or one person changing so dramatically that the old pattern can't hold.

New relationships feel exciting because they're frequency exploratory.

You haven't locked into a pattern yet. Every interaction is testing what frequency the relationship will stabilize around. This is the honeymoon phase on an energetic level.

You're sampling different frequencies to see what resonates. Once the relationship stabilizes, usually within 3-9 months, the frequency locks and becomes the baseline.

After that, the relationship functions to maintain that baseline, not explore new ones.

(Isis is the archetype of resonance, protection, and divine reflection, her wings symbolically enfold and amplify whatever energy is present).

You can identify your actual frequency by looking at who stays and who leaves.

The people who stay long-term are resonant with your baseline, not your aspirational frequency.

If you want to know what you're really broadcasting, look at who's still around after two years. They're the ones whose field is compatible with yours as it actually is.

The ones who left weren't wrong for you. They were resonant with a different frequency, and when they sensed your actual baseline, they naturally drifted away.

There's a specific phenomenon where people choose partners who match their unhealed frequency.

You're broadcasting from a wound, and you attract someone whose wound is complementary. This creates intensity but not health. The relationship feels magnetic because the wounds are interlocking, but it's ultimately unsustainable because it's organized around pathology rather than wholeness.

When you heal the wound, the frequency shifts, and the relationship either evolves or dissolves. Most dissolve because they had no foundation beyond the wound resonance.

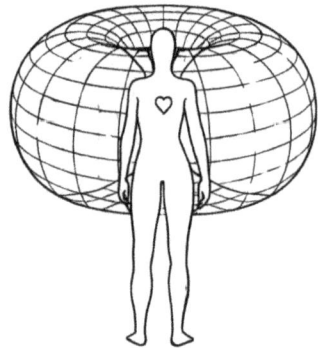

(As Tesla used resonance to transmit energy, you use it to attract, not by chasing, but by sustaining your frequency).

Upgrading your relational frequency requires upgrading your baseline first, not trying to attract different people with the same frequency.

You can't relationship-hop your way into a better frequency. Every new relationship will eventually reveal your baseline and organize around it.

The only way to attract genuinely different relationship dynamics is to become genuinely different at the frequency level. Change the broadcast, and different receivers start picking up the signal. Try to attract different receivers with the same broadcast, and you'll keep recreating the same dynamics with new faces.

RELATIONAL FREQUENCY

*Your frequency affects **every connection you make.***

Aligned energy strengthens relationships and influence.

Discordant signals cause friction and breakdown.

This is social energy dynamics.

Mastering relational frequency means tuning your state,

so your interactions build support and momentum.

Your environment holds memory.
Not metaphorically, but energetically.
Every thought, emotion, and event leaves an imprint in the space around it, the same way sound leaves vibration in the air.

Ancient philosophers called this the astral residue, the subtle record of human experience that lingers in matter.

Walk into a room where people have been arguing and you feel it instantly, even if the argument ended hours ago. Walk into a place where someone has been creating or praying, and you feel that too. The environment isn't just reflecting energy. It's storing it, layering it, and transmitting it back. You're not just in the space. The space is in you.

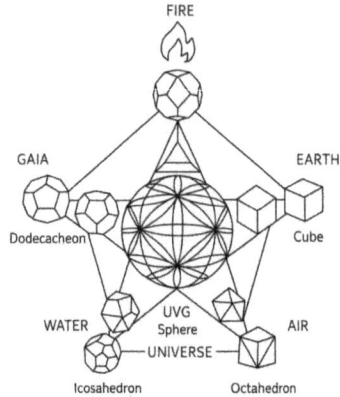

Most people underestimate how much their surroundings shape their internal state.

They think consciousness operates independently, but no one evolves in a vacuum.

You are constantly exchanging frequency with the field around you. Try to hold a calm, coherent state in a space that's been saturated with stress for years, and you'll feel the drag immediately.

The field resists new order until it's re-patterned. It's like trying to have a quiet conversation in a nightclub, possible, but energetically expensive.

(The moon governs the subconscious, just as it governs the tides, shaping mood, memory, and the unseen movements of the mind).

Every space becomes a frequency anchor.

Your bedroom, your car, your workspace, these are not neutral zones. They're energetic ecosystems that absorb your most repeated emotional tone. A home that has held worry for years becomes magnetized to it. A workspace that's been used for focus accumulates precision. If you've been tense at your desk long enough, that tension is now woven into the air.

You can enter the space feeling clear and within minutes find yourself mirroring the old state. It's not weakness. It's entrainment. The space is echoing what it's learned.

(As above, so below, the outer reflects the inner, and the pattern won't change until the vibration does).

(This Ka preservation ritual isn't just ancient art, it's a symbolic blueprint for frequency alignment. Your next level isn't sustained by desire alone, but by the structure you build to hold its signal).

This is why certain rooms, homes, or cities feel different the moment you arrive.

Every environment carries the residue of the consciousness that shaped it. Some spaces feel heavy because they're saturated with unresolved emotion. Others feel light because coherence has been maintained there.

When you move into a new place, you're not starting fresh, you're inheriting an existing vibrational record.

Until you establish your own frequency through repeated, coherent states, the old one continues to influence you.

You can rewrite environmental frequency, but not through superficial ritual alone. Sage, sound, or crystals may temporarily shift surface vibration, but lasting change comes from consistent broadcast.

The environment obeys the most dominant and sustained frequency within it. Hold calm, focus, and clarity in the same space long enough, and the walls themselves begin to resonate differently. Ancient temples were designed for this reason, their geometry and silence amplified stable vibration.

You don't need a temple. You just need consistency. Thirty days of coherent signal in one room begins to reprogram it.

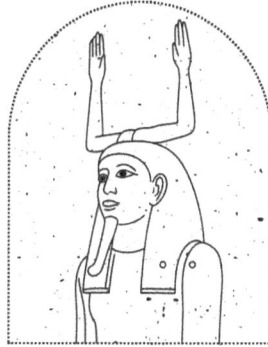

(The Ka, Egypt's (and your) energetic double, needed a sacred space to survive. Just like your future self needs an environment that supports its frequency).

(Tombs weren't just burial sites. They were energetic chambers, designed to nourish and sustain the Ka so it could live on after death).

The most powerful way to shift environmental energy is through completion and order.

Physical clutter is energetic clutter, matter frozen mid-decision. The corner stacked with unopened mail isn't just disorganized; it's broadcasting procrastination. The clothes you'll never wear are broadcasting avoidance.

Every incomplete thing in your space is an open loop leaking energy. Clearing it isn't decoration; it's restoration.

When you finish what's unfinished and release what's stagnant, the environment stops mirroring delay and begins amplifying direction.

ENVIRONMENTAL FREQUENCY

Your environment reflects your **dominant frequency.**

Stable fields attract aligned energy and opportunity.

Chaotic surroundings disrupt your signal and progress.

This is not coincidence.

Mastering environmental frequency means cultivating coherence,

so your space supports your intent and growth.

CALIBRATION CARD

Steps

Write one clear statement that represents the energy you are choosing to transmit from this point forward.

Not a hope. A broadcast.

Make it short. Make it specific.

Write it as if the shift has already happened, and you're just holding the signal.

IMPRINT YOUR ENVIRONMENT

Cut it out, paste it somewhere common. Imprint your environment. Use this card as a daily reference to hold the outcome in mind and emotion, until it becomes familiar.

(Write as if it is already happening. Be clear, not vague.)

```



..........................................................................................


..........................................................................................


..........................................................................................


```

Example prompts:
- *"I move with certainty. The path unfolds in response."*
- *"My clarity attracts aligned outcomes without force."*
- *"I radiate peace. And what I meet mirrors it."*

SECTION IV: THE CREATION PROTOCOL

Most people think creation starts when something shows up. It doesn't. It starts the moment the field receives clear instruction.

Before the job appears, before the relationship forms, before the money moves - there's a transmission. Your field broadcasts a signal into the unseen, and if that signal is coherent enough, dense enough, stable enough, the physical catches up.

What you call manifestation is just matter confirming what energy already organized. The lag between broadcast and evidence is where most people give up. They think nothing's happening. Everything's happening. You just can't see it yet.

(Aztec temples weren't just structures, they were energetic instruments. Aligned with constellations and cosmic cycles, they turned ritual into signal, proving that creation begins through coherence, not appearance).

Thought provides the image. Emotion provides the charge. But repetition is what makes it stick.

You don't create something once and watch it appear. You install the instruction through consistency. Every time you return to the same internal state, the same vision, the same frequency - you're reinforcing the signal.

The field doesn't respond to wishes or fleeting intentions. It responds to patterns. To what you become, not what you want. The loop is simple: think it, feel it, repeat it until your system accepts it as real. Then the external has no choice but to match.

(Om is the first frequency, the primordial sound from which all creation emerged, symbolizing the bridge between the unseen and the seen.).

This isn't new age nonsense. It's ancient science dressed in modern language.

The Egyptians called it heka - the power to shape reality through sound and vibration. The Hebrews understood dabar as the word that doesn't just describe, it causes. Hermetic philosophy said "All is Mind" because they knew consciousness precedes form.

Every tradition pointed to the same mechanism: what you hold internally with enough intensity and consistency becomes what you experience externally. The instruction doesn't start with your mouth. It starts with your state. The resonance you carry before the thought even forms.

(Hermes Trismegistus, the symbolic voice of Hermetic wisdom, taught that the universe is mental, that all creation begins in thought, and the mind is the key that shapes reality).

(Reality spirals outward from a single internal instruction. This diagram is not theory, it's a structure of cause).

Think back to your biggest breakthroughs. They didn't come from trying harder. They came after something inside you shifted. You stopped hoping and started knowing. You stopped asking and started assuming.

That internal shift preceded the external evidence by days, weeks, sometimes months. But the shift came first. Always.

That's how instruction works. It's not loud. It's not dramatic. It's a quiet internal lock-in, a resolve that doesn't waver. Once that signal stabilizes, reality reorganizes to meet it.

Not because you forced it.
Because the field had a clear directive.

But here's the problem: most people are broadcasting mixed signals. They visualize success while feeling like a fraud. They want love while expecting rejection. They affirm abundance while their body holds scarcity.

The field doesn't care about your affirmations. It reads your actual state.

If there's contradiction between what you want and what you believe you deserve, the instruction isn't clear. The field receives static. And static doesn't manifest. It scatters. You have to close the gap. Thought, feeling, and embodiment must align. When they do, the instruction becomes undeniable.

(The Rebis visually encodes this truth: You cannot issue two conflicting instructions to the field. Only when internal unity is achieved does the instruction become executable).

(The Seal of Inner Law, when thought, feeling, and will align, the instruction becomes law, crystallizing into form, and compelling the field to respond).

This isn't about hope or faith in the traditional sense. It's about causation. You're not praying to an external force and hoping it responds.

You're encoding an instruction into your field through repetition, emotion, and coherence. That instruction doesn't vanish after one visualization. It accumulates. It compounds. It builds until it reaches critical mass, and then it collapses into form.

You're not part of creation. You are the interface through which it operates. What you hold inside with consistency becomes what the field holds outside in physical form.

THE INSTRUCTION LOOP

*Creation begins the
moment a signal
stabilizes within.*

*Not when
something appears,
but when
**instruction is
sustained**.*

*Thought gives
direction. Emotion
gives power.
Repetition makes
it real.*

*This is not
mysticism.
It's mechanics.*

*Your field
broadcasts what
you hold.*

And life reflects it.

The difference between someone who creates once and someone who creates consistently isn't talent. It's endurance.

Most people can spike their frequency for a day, maybe a week. They get inspired, they feel aligned, they broadcast clean signal. Then life happens. A bill comes. A rejection lands. Someone criticizes them. And they're back to baseline within hours.

Frequency mastery isn't about avoiding disruption. It's about returning faster. The master doesn't avoid getting knocked off center. They just don't stay there. They notice the drop, recalibrate, and return to signal. That's the skill. Not perfection. Recovery speed.

(Hermanubis stands still, unmoved by the world around him, because he knows the signal is not proven by instant results, but by unwavering continuity).

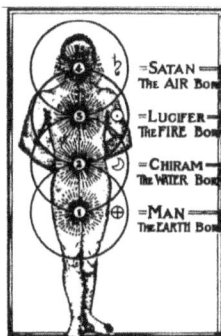

Your nervous system has momentum. If you've been running anxiety for ten years, it has grooves. Deep ones.

When you try to hold a new frequency, you're not just choosing it once. You're redirecting momentum. And momentum doesn't reverse instantly.

This is why the first two weeks feel like you're forcing it. You are. You're creating new grooves while the old ones are still pulling. But around day fourteen, something shifts. The new pattern starts feeling less like effort and more like option. By day thirty, it's becoming automatic. By day ninety, it's your new default. The early resistance isn't failure. It's friction. And friction means you're actually changing something.

THE MACROCOSMIC MAN
The Four Births Out of the Body of Brahma

Most people think frequency work is about maintaining a feeling. It's not. Feelings fluctuate. That's biology.

Frequency mastery is about maintaining direction regardless of feeling. You can be tired and still hold the frequency. You can be frustrated and still hold the frequency.

Because the frequency isn't an emotion. It's a decision about what's true. When you decide something is true and you hold that decision through contradicting evidence, through emotional turbulence, through external delays - that's when the field recognizes you're serious. Anyone can hold a frequency when it feels good. The Operator holds it when it doesn't.

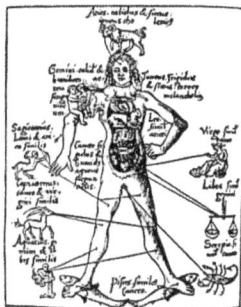

(Just as each astrological sign governs a part of the body, each thought governs a region of your field. To hold a signal is to bring the whole system into agreement).

There's a phenomenon called frequency drift. You start the day aligned, but by noon you've drifted back to old patterns without noticing.

This happens because your environment, your conversations, your habitual thoughts all have their own momentum. They pull you back to familiar frequencies.

Frequency mastery requires checkpoints. Not obsessive monitoring. Strategic recalibration. Set three moments each day where you pause and ask: what frequency am I actually holding right now? Not what you intended to hold. What you're actually broadcasting. Most people discover they drifted hours ago. The checkpoint isn't about judgment. It's about course correction before the drift becomes a day, a week, a month.

(As Isis pours the current into the world, so must you become the vessel that sustains it, not temporarily, but until the outer reshapes to match the inner).

Attention doesn't just focus energy. It amplifies whatever it touches. When you give attention to doubt, doubt grows. When you give attention to the old story, the old story strengthens. This is why mastering frequency requires attention discipline. Not suppression. Redirection.

You're not pretending doubt doesn't exist. You're choosing not to feed it with focus. Every time you catch yourself replaying the old narrative and you consciously redirect to the new one, you're not just thinking differently. You're rewiring the neural pathways that generate your field. The brain follows attention. Attention shapes frequency. Frequency organizes reality. It's a chain. And you control the first link.

(The Sphinx represents the final gate of mastery. It tests whether your inner signal is theory or truth, guarding the path that only aligned consciousness can pass).

Frequency holding becomes effortless once it stops being something you do and becomes something you are.

At first, you consciously redirect your focus, reminding yourself of the signal whenever you drift. But with steady repetition, usually after sixty to ninety days, the signal imprints into your nervous system and becomes automatic. It turns into your new baseline, a stable broadcast your body maintains without thought.

That's when manifestation accelerates, not because the field suddenly changes, but because your signal finally holds enough consistency for reality to organize around it.

(In Ancient Egypt, the sistrum was not just an instrument, it was a tool of frequency regulation, used to hold resonance in alignment with divine instruction).

FREQUENCY MASTERY

Clarity is easy.
**Consistency is
creation.**

*Frequency must be
held to translate into
form.*

*Emotion stabilizes
the signal.*
Focus maintains it.
Time tests it.

*This isn't energy
work.*

*It's vibratory
alignment.*

*The field does not
reward desire.*

**It reflects
endurance.**

FREQUENCY MASTERY

Describe your mastery clearly:

- *How are you consciously controlling and sustaining your frequency?*

....

....

....

....

- *What practices and mindsets support your frequency mastery?*

....

....

....

....

Example prompts:
- *I maintain steady focus that shapes my experience.*
- *My energy remains clear and resilient under pressure.*
- *I choose thoughts that keep my vibration aligned with my goals.*
- *I effortlessly return to center when distractions arise.*

Most people interpret endings as evidence they failed at something. A job loss, a relationship ending, a carefully constructed plan falling through - they see it as proof they did something wrong or weren't good enough. But frequency doesn't happen through addition, it happens through shedding what can no longer match the new vibration.

When you genuinely elevate your baseline frequency, everything still operating at the old level becomes unstable, not because those things are bad or wrong, but because they're frequency-mismatched with where you're going. Your field is reorganizing itself around new coherence, and anything that can't match that coherence has to exit the system.

(Ma'at is the vibrational coherence between internal truth and external order. To "live in Ma'at" means to align your actions, thoughts, and heart with this underlying order).

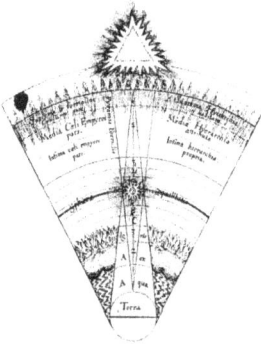

(Reality doesn't fall apart, it funnels into form. This Hermetic diagram reveals what quantum physics calls collapse: infinite potential narrowing into one stabilized path).

There's a specific type of collapse that happens right before major breakthrough, and if you don't understand it you'll interpret it as failure and quit right before success. You're holding the new frequency with real consistency, you're doing everything the protocol says, everything feels like it's finally working - then suddenly multiple areas of your life fall apart simultaneously.

This isn't random chaos or bad luck, it's what's called compression collapse, where the old frequency makes one final concentrated attempt to pull you back to familiar territory. Your entire system is being tested with one clear question: will you revert to old patterns when pressure hits, or will you hold the new signal through the chaos?

Collapse reveals where your attachments still live, which is valuable information most people don't want to see.
You think you're ready for the new level until something from the old level gets taken away, then you realize how much you were still secretly holding onto it for security.

That identity you claimed you'd released? If its collapse triggers existential crisis, you hadn't genuinely let it go yet. Collapse shows you precisely where your stated frequency doesn't match your actual attachment level, and this isn't judgment or criticism, it's diagnostic data. Now you know where the real work is, not in affirming the new reality you want, but in genuinely releasing the old one you're still gripping.

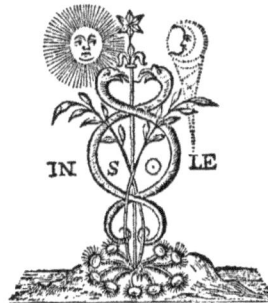

(True transformation doesn't begin with elevation, it begins with unraveling. What rises must first shed what no longer aligns).

(Tarot doesn't predict the future, it reveals the present. Cards like The Tower reflect your current state of consciousness, making the invisible visible through symbolic selection).

Some collapses aren't about loss or failure.

They're about creating room for what's trying to arrive. Your field has limited capacity, and when it's crowded with old attachments, relationships, commitments, patterns, there's no bandwidth left for what aligns with your new frequency. Collapse clears that space.

It empties what's incompatible so something coherent can take form. That's why major gain often follows loss: the job ends and the better one appears, the relationship dissolves and the right one surfaces.

The field doesn't stack realities; it replaces them.

There's also internal collapse that isn't caused by outside events. The identity you've been performing starts feeling false, the goals you've been chasing lose meaning, and the life you imagined stops exciting you.

This isn't failure or depression, it's frequency mismatch. Who you're becoming no longer fits the blueprint you're still running. Your signal has evolved, but your system is trying to operate on outdated code, and it begins rejecting it.

Collapse isn't punishment; it's confirmation that you've outgrown the frequency that built your old reality.

(This image depicts the alignment of higher will over lower nature, the symbolic slaying of distortion by clarity. Pegasus is to move in elevated frequency; to pierce the beast is to collapse what no longer resonates).

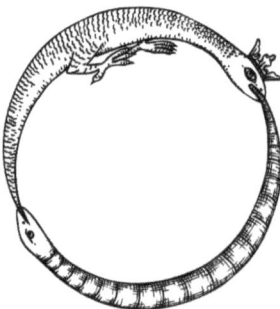

The only way through collapse is through it. Don't resist or rush to rebuild what's falling. You can't outthink it, bypass it, or mask it with false positivity.

Let the process finish before constructing anything new. Most people panic mid-collapse and try to reconstruct the old framework, which only prolongs the disorder. The field is clearing space with surgical precision, let it work. Keep holding your new frequency, but don't interfere with what's being dismantled. It's not destruction; it's preparation.

What's aligned will remain. What's gone in frequency will soon disappear in form.

COLLAPSE AS CALIBRATION

What breaks down
is what can't hold
your new signal.

Collapse isn't
punishment.

It's pattern
correction.

Your field is
reorganizing.

Not around
preference, but
around precision.

This isn't
destruction.
It's refinement.

Frequency deletes
what no longer
fits.

Command State isn't something you learn from scratch, it's something you remember.

You've been there before, in moments where you moved with absolute certainty and reality bent around you. But then you dropped back into hoping, trying, wondering if things would work out.

Command State is the shift from negotiating with possibility to operating from decision. Not arrogant decision that needs to announce itself, but clear decision that's already complete internally. When you move from that place, resistance stops being relevant. You're not overcoming obstacles, you're reconfiguring the field so they don't form.

(The angel represents your higher self in full alignment, wings extended as the embodiment of elevated frequency).

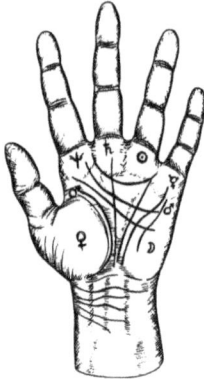

Command State has a distinct frequency signature different from confidence or belief.

Confidence says "I think I can," belief says "I know this can work," but Command says nothing because it expects.

When you're in genuine Command State, you're not generating emotion to convince yourself or affirming to override doubt. You're operating from a reality where the outcome is already handled.

This isn't delusion - it's identity-level decision. The field responds to identity frequency, not effort, and when your identity has absorbed the outcome as fact, your field broadcasts pure instruction automatically.

Most people confuse Command State with control, thinking it means forcing reality through willpower.

It's the opposite. Command emerges when you're so internally aligned you stop needing to control how anything unfolds. You set the frequency and let the field organize details.

This requires trust most people lack because they want to see the path before committing to the destination. Command means committing so completely that the path forms in response. You're not controlling how, you're broadcasting what so clearly that the how organizes itself around your signal.

("We can only escape from the world by outgrowing the world")
- Manly P Hall

Your body enters Command State before your mind catches up.

Watch someone operating from Command, their breathing is slower, deeper, anchored. Their movements carry weight without force. They don't rush because rushing implies doubt, and they don't over-explain because explanation implies defense. Even their silence carries instruction.

This is why presence is more powerful than words. Words come from mind, presence comes from field, and when that field broadcasts Command State, people feel it before you speak.

(This is the mind as a temple: built on pillars of clarity, upheld by discipline, and crowned with intent. When your inner architecture is stable, reality conforms to its structure.).

Command State cannot coexist with need. The moment you need the outcome, you've dropped into hope.

Need creates desperation, desperation fragments coherence. Command operates from internal sufficiency - not having everything you want, but being complete regardless of circumstances.

This is the paradox: you get what you want when you no longer need it. Needing means your frequency is organized around lack. Being complete means your frequency is organized around wholeness that naturally attracts. Command isn't about filling a hole, it's about becoming so complete that what you want finds you.

You don't maintain Command State permanently - you'll drop out regularly. Something will trigger doubt, activate conditioning, or land in an unhealed spot.

The difference between dabblers and Operators isn't that Operators never drop out - it's that they return faster. They notice the drop, recalibrate, and step back into Command without making it mean failure.

The drop is feedback. "Oh, I'm in reaction mode", return to Command. The practice isn't perfection, it's conscious return. Every return strengthens the pathway until Command becomes default.

(Command State is the internal compass set to coherence, not seeking direction, but issuing it).

COMMAND STATE

Command state is
**where clarity meets
power.**

*It's the place you
step beyond reaction
into control.*

*Here, your focus
sharpens, your
energy condenses.*

*You don't just
respond,* **you direct.**

*Old patterns lose
grip as you claim
your center.*

*This isn't rigid rule;
it's fluid mastery.*

In command state,

**reality bends to
your steady will.**

Most people run programming they didn't choose and never questioned.

Parents, teachers, culture, trauma - they installed beliefs about what's possible, what you deserve, how reality works. You've been operating from inherited code without examining if it's true or just conditioning.

The Operator Identity begins when you recognize the code isn't fixed - you can rewrite it. Not through positive thinking layered on top, but by recognizing your current identity is a frequency structure you inherited and mistook for who you are. You are the awareness that can choose different programming, and when you own that, the system becomes programmable.

(Atum is the ancient Egyptian god of self-creation, the one who emerged from nothing and shaped reality by will alone).

Identity determines what your system allows, functioning as a permission filter. If your identity says "I struggle with money," your field won't permit sustained wealth. Not because the universe punishes you, but because identity only allows matching experiences.

This is why working on beliefs without shifting identity doesn't create lasting change. You can affirm abundance for years, but if your identity hasn't shifted from "person who struggles" to "person for whom resources flow," your field rejects abundance because it doesn't match.

The Operator doesn't fix individual beliefs - they upgrade identity, and beliefs automatically reconfigure.

(The Renaissance heraldic eagle symbolizes sovereign will, divine authority, and elevated perception).

Every initiatory system understood this. Hermetic initiation wasn't about learning information - it was identity transformation.

You weren't taught you could access divine power, you were initiated into remembering you are divine power focused through human form. Kabbalists didn't teach manifestation techniques - they taught that Ein Sof, the infinite, is expressing itself as you.

Your individuality isn't separate from source, it's source experiencing itself through one focal point. When you stop identifying as separate from creative force and start identifying as its localized expression, everything changes. You're not asking creation to help you, you are creation directing itself.

(This symbol represents the sacred secretion (Christos), as it rises up the spine, activating the pineal gland and awakening higher consciousness).

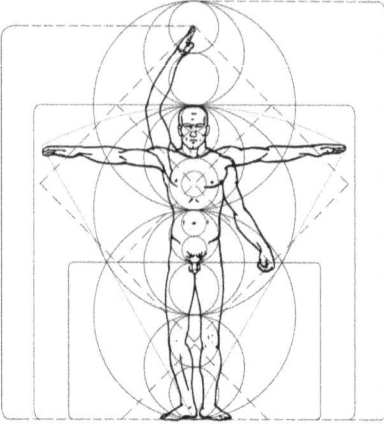

The Operator Identity isn't egoic. Ego says "I'm special, I'm better." The Operator says "I'm source-localized, and so is everyone else, they've just forgotten." There's no superiority, just recognition.

You're not more than anyone, you're just awake to what you are. And what you are is consciousness using a nervous system to interface with physical reality.

Your thoughts are directives. Your emotions are calibration signals. Your attention is the tool through which consciousness shapes form.
Once you see this, you can't unsee it or go back to operating like a victim.

Most people live as if reality happens to them. The Operator knows reality happens through them.

There's no external authority determining your experience - only your frequency broadcast and the field's response.

This is terrifying because it removes every excuse. If you're creating through frequency, you can't blame parents, circumstances, or luck. But it's profoundly liberating. If you've been creating unconsciously, you can create consciously. Nothing external has to change for your experience to shift - you just change the frequency you broadcast, and that's within your control.

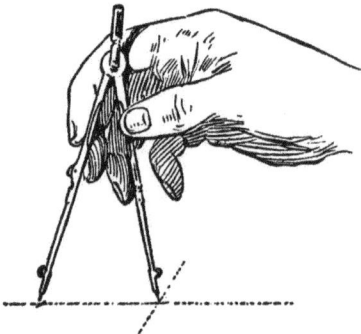

The shift to Operator Identity is instantaneous, not gradual.

You're either operating as effect or as cause. No middle ground. One day you're hoping reality treats you well, the next you realize you're directing reality through your field. The shift happens in a moment, but stabilizing it takes practice.

You'll fluctuate, dropping into victim consciousness when triggered. But now you'll notice, and noticing is everything. When you notice you've dropped into effect mode, you can return to cause mode. You're not becoming the Operator, you already are. You're just remembering.

THE OPERATOR IDENTITY

The Operator Identity is owning your role as **creator and controller.**

You're no longer a passenger but **the pilot of your frequency.**

Every thought, feeling, and choice feeds your signal.

This is not passive, it's active engagement.

Stepping into this identity means embracing responsibility,

so your reality flows from deliberate design,

not random chance.

THE OPERATOR IDENTITY

ASSUME THE ROLE. ISSUE THE FREQUENCY.

Set your transmission point:

- *What identity are you broadcasting into the field right now?*

....

....

....

....

- *What assumptions are locked into that identity?*

....

....

....

....

Example prompts:
- *I'm not waiting for alignment, I generate it through signal.*
- *I assume influence, structure bends to who I've already become.*
- *I've stopped asking, the field responds to what I've already claimed.*
- *Reality reflects me, because I configure it with precision, not hope.*

Your imagination isn't optional, you're using it constantly, whether consciously or not.

The question isn't whether to imagine, it's what you're imagining by default. Most people's imagination runs on autopilot, replaying worst-case scenarios, rehearsing conflicts that haven't happened, visualizing failure. Because the subconscious doesn't distinguish between imagined and real, every image becomes instruction.
You're programming outcomes without realizing it.
Imagination Protocol isn't about adding a new practice, it's about redirecting the imagination you're already running, from unconscious rehearsal of problems to deliberate construction of creation.

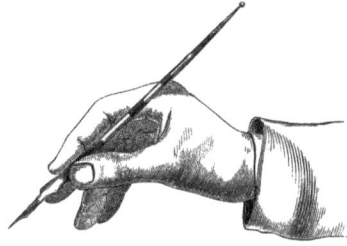

"The Imagination is the most powerful most miraculous inconceivably powerful force that the world's ever known."

- Napoleon Hill

The subconscious accepts images faster than language, which is why affirmations alone rarely work.

You can say "I am wealthy" a thousand times, but if your imagery shows you struggling, the image wins. Your imagination is the direct line to subconscious programming. When you imagine vividly, your nervous system experiences it as real - heart rate changes, breathing adjusts, biochemistry shifts. The body doesn't know the difference between rehearsal and reality.

This is why athletes who visualize improve almost as much as those who physically practice - the nervous system treats both as real training.

There's a difference between fantasy and instruction.

Fantasy is imagining something you don't believe is possible. It feels good temporarily, then creates emptiness. Instruction is imagining something your system accepts as achievable. It doesn't feel like escape, it feels like preview. The difference isn't content, it's belief underneath. You can imagine wealth as fantasy - "wouldn't it be nice if..." - or as instruction - "this is what's coming." Same image, different frequency.

One is hoping, one is encoding. The Operator doesn't fantasize. They preview outcomes their identity has permission to experience.

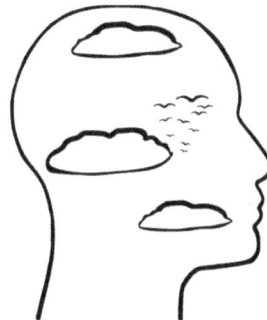

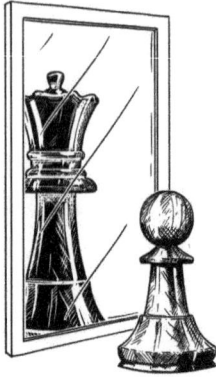

Imagination works best in first person, present tense. Not "I will have this," but "I have this now." The more sensorially rich, the better. What do you see? Hear? Feel physically? What temperature? What smells?

The more detail, the more your nervous system treats it as actual experience. Actual experience creates neural pathways that become highways your reality travels to meet you.

This isn't magic, it's neurology. Your brain can't tell the difference between vivid imagination and reality, so consistent imagination pre-builds the neural infrastructure for the reality you're calling in.

Most people imagine once, feel good, then forget about it. That's dabbling. Imagination Protocol means scheduled rehearsal - same vision, same detail, same frequency, every day. Preferably twice: morning to set frequency, night to embed before sleep when your subconscious is receptive.

This isn't about duration, it's consistency. Five minutes daily for thirty days rewires you more than one hour once because the subconscious learns through repetition.

Every time you return to the same imagined reality, you strengthen the signal, telling your system: this is where we're going.

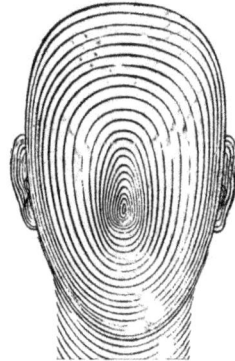

Imagination isn't separate from action, it's the blueprint that makes action effective.

When you imagine first, actions become naturally aligned because your system is already oriented there. You don't force right action, you naturally move toward what matches the imagined reality. This is why people who visualize take better action than those who just hustle - they're not figuring out what to do, they're following the pull toward what exists in their imagination. Imagination creates the template, action fills it in.

Without the template, action is random. With it, action is magnetic because you're working from a reality that exists in frequency, pulling it into form.

IMAGINATION PROTOCOL

Imagination is not escape.
It's interface.

What you hold in vision becomes structural in the field.

The ether doesn't respond to fleeting thought, **it responds to sustained frequency**.

If you hold it in your mind long enough, it must become reality.

That is not hope.
It is law.

Imagination isn't a distraction. It's how instructions are built.

Not daydreaming,
design.

FIELD CLOSURE: THE REMEMBERING

You are not separate from the universe.

You are its localized expression, encoded with the same intelligence that governs galaxies, atoms, and the precise timing of seasons. The same field that births stars is pulsing through your nervous system right now.

You are not observing reality from outside it like a spectator watching a screen. You are projecting it from within, constantly, through every thought you sustain and every frequency you hold. The separation you feel is the only illusion you ever fell for, and the moment you see through it, everything changes.

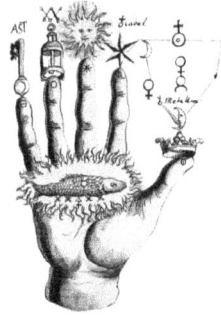

(The Hand of the Macro-Microcosm", a Hermetic symbol showing that the human system mirrors cosmic law. You're not separate from the universe. You're configured to direct it).

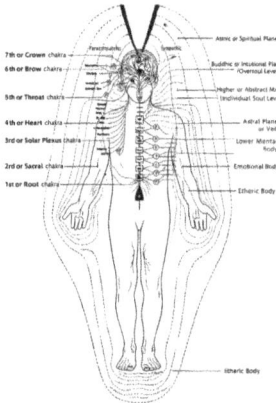

Everything is electromagnetic.

The chair beneath you, the thought moving through your mind, the emotion rising in your chest - all of it is vibration at different densities and speeds.

Vibration is not metaphor or spiritual language, it is the base structure of physical existence that science keeps confirming. And your body is its most refined instrument, capable of tuning to any frequency and holding it long enough to collapse probability into form. You were born as transmitter, receiver, and creator simultaneously. The question was never whether you have this capacity. The question is whether you remember you do.

This is not esoteric idealism or religious mythology.

It is the literal architecture of how reality operates. You are infinite consciousness localized, condensed into human form to navigate three-dimensional experience and create within specific limitations.

You have the capacity to bend probability fields, alter timelines, and instruct matter into new configurations. Not through force or willpower, but through sustained frequency that's coherent enough to override default patterns. Through signal. Through broadcast. Through becoming so internally aligned that the external has no choice but to reorganize around you.

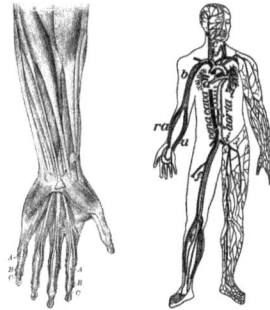

(Your body is the instrument through which consciousness directs frequency into form).

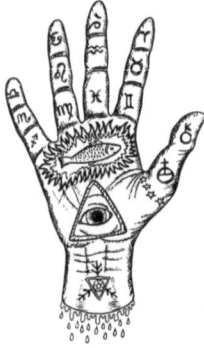

(A Hermetic diagram symbolizing the awakening of man as a conduit of universal forces).

You're not here to wait for permission or for conditions to improve. You're here to remember what you already are, and through that remembering, evolve beyond inherited limits.

Life is designed for growth through contrast and feedback. Resistance isn't punishment; it's information showing where your frequency is misaligned. Delay isn't denial; it's the field calibrating to your signal. Collapse isn't failure; it's correction, clearing what can't coexist with your new baseline.

Everything responds to your broadcast. Shift the frequency at the source, and reality reorganizes around it.

You were never meant to chase outcomes like someone running after a bus that keeps pulling away. You were meant to tune your frequency until outcomes have no choice but to find you.

Manifestation isn't about pleading with an external force to grant your wishes. It's aligning your field so precisely that probability collapses in your favor because you've become a vibrational match for what you seek.

As you apply this consistently, you won't just believe it works, you'll see it working. Patterns will reorganize, and circumstances will bend in ways that seem like coincidence but are actually precision, not because the world changed, but because you did.

(A symbolic wheel aligning the twelve constellations with regions of the human body, from Aries at the head to Pisces at the feet. The body becomes the axis of celestial influence).

This is your power.

It's the ability to encode the field with clear intention, to hold a vision so precisely that it solidifies into form, and to transmit truth without distortion.

This isn't wishful thinking; it's the measurable physics of consciousness.

The law is simple: what you consistently sustain within your field must appear in your experience. The delay is only the gap between the signal you send and the coherence required to hold it without contradiction. Once coherence locks, form follows.

To remember is to awaken what's been dormant, to stop shrinking in a reality that mirrors your every broadcast.

It's withdrawing energy from false stories about limitation and outdated identities that never fit who you are.

You are not your past or your conditioning. You are consciousness experiencing itself through your point in space and time.

Whether you think you can or can't, both become true, because thought configures reality.

All is mind, and mind is all.

Every frequency you emit is a choice, whether you're making it consciously or not.

A directive to the field. A statement of what you're aligned with. Creation is not something that happens to you while you hope for the best. It is something that happens through you as the localized point of creative power.

$$a^2 + b^2 = c^2$$

(The Pythagorean Theorem is more than math, it's a symbol of aligned forces. When all sides are in proportion, form becomes stable. So does reality).

The more you remember this and operate from it, the more precise your projection becomes and the more responsive reality gets. What used to feel random starts feeling organized. What used to feel impossible starts feeling inevitable. Clear. Obedient to your internal configuration because you're finally broadcasting without static.

You are the universe expressing itself through self-aware consciousness.

The operator of your reality. The architect of your experience. The broadcaster determining what becomes form.

The illusion was never powerlessness, only forgetting. You spent years giving that power to circumstances and others.

Remembering restores authorship. Now that you see how creation works, you no longer hope it aligns, you direct it, consciously and deliberately, knowing reality was designed to respond to you.

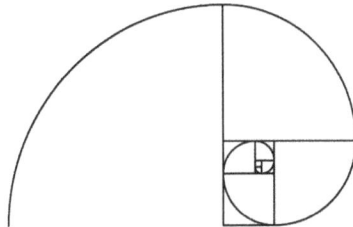

(World = Whirled. "All Is Atum").

THE REMEMBERING

You were never
waiting for a sign.

You were the sign.

Not a seeker,
A broadcaster.

Not an echo.
The origin.

What you hold,
you build.

What you are,
becomes.

Creation isn't
outside of you.

It follows you.

Now you know.
And from here on,
everything responds.

You now understand how your
frequency shapes your reality.
But knowing means nothing
without action.

Every thought, every feeling, every
choice builds your world. You control
the signal. You control the outcome.

Keep this clear. Stay deliberate.
Own your power.

This is just the start.
Your reality is yours to command.

GLOSSARY

Energy (3) – The essential source; the raw, infinite force behind all existence, representing the subtle essence of thoughts and emotions fueling creation.

Frequency (6) – The measured flow and rate at which energy moves within you, organizing and structuring your internal state to form a coherent signal.

Vibration (9) – The manifested expression of energy and frequency in motion; the final, dynamic form that shapes your experience and reality.

Signal – The coherent pattern of thought and emotion you broadcast into the field/universe, shaping your experience.

Frequency Calibration – The process of tuning and stabilizing your emotional and mental states to maintain a consistent internal signal.

Resonance – The principle that like frequencies attract; your internal vibration draws corresponding external experiences.

Energetic Gravity – The natural pull created by your core frequency, attracting aligned people, opportunities, and circumstances.

Thought Loop / Emotional Loop – A repetitive mental or emotional pattern that influences your subconscious programming and external reality.

Belief Layer – The foundational subconscious convictions that govern how your internal signals are formed and interpreted.

Signal Interference – Internal contradictions, distractions, or conflicting emotions that weaken or distort your frequency.

Embodied Frequency – The way your physical state and body language broadcast your internal frequency to the world.

Energy Manipulation – The conscious control and direction of your internal energy to manifest desired outcomes.

External Navigation – The skill of interacting with and influencing your external environment through mastery of your internal frequency.

Command State – A focused mental and emotional condition where you actively direct your internal frequency to influence reality.

Operator Identity – The conscious role you assume as the creator and controller of your frequency and experiences.

Frequency Mastery – The ongoing practice of maintaining clarity, coherence, and control over your internal frequency.

Law of Resonance – The universal principle stating that similar frequencies attract each other, shaping your external world.

Energy Leak – The unintentional loss or dispersion of your internal energy that weakens your frequency's power.

Feedback Loop – The process where your internal frequency influences external events, which in turn reinforce or alter your frequency.

Subconscious Operator – The part of the subconscious mind that automatically manages your frequency based on ingrained beliefs and habits.

Frequency Collapse – A breakdown in internal coherence causing scattered energy and weakened manifestation power.

*"Whatever the mind can conceive
and believe, it can achieve."*

— Napoleon Hill

THE JOURNEY CONTINUES

Find us **@accuratethought** on
Instagram and TikTok.

We break down the mechanics
through practical, repeatable
content on frequency, coherence,
and internal alignment.

If this book landed with you,
capture the moment and tag us.
We amplify readers who engage
with the work.

Frequency recognizes readiness.
You're now part of the
transmission.